The Independent Director

To Averil, Chloë and Gail

THE
INDEPENDENT
DIRECTOR

*Handbook and guide to
corporate governance*

**William Houston
and
Nigel Lewis**

BUTTERWORTH
HEINEMANN

Butterworth-Heinemann Ltd
Linacre House, Jordan Hill, Oxford OX2 8DP

PART OF REED INTERNATIONAL BOOKS

OXFORD   LONDON   BOSTON
MUNICH   NEW DELHI   SINGAPORE   SYDNEY
TOKYO   TORONTO   WELLINGTON

First published 1992

British Library Cataloguing in Publication Data
Houston, William
    The Independent Director: Handbook and
    Guide to Corporate Governance
    I. Title II. Lewis, Nigel
    658.4

ISBN 0 7506 0659 2

Photoset by Deltatype Limited, Ellesmere Port
Printed and bound in Great Britain by Clays, St Ives plc

Contents

vi *Contents*

Foreword

Following the spectacular crashes and corporate upsets of the 1980s and early 1990s, the question of corporate governance has become extremely topical.

The essence of the question, of course, is all to do with protecting the interests of shareholders and securing the health of the company.

The big institutions inevitably exert the greatest muscle, but they act in the interests of small individual shareholders too. Are the top people in a company paying themselves too much? Does the Board have a clear, realistic and achievable strategy for the future? How are expansion plans or developments to be financed? Are the company's accounting practices, systems and audits providing all the information which might affect investors' views and, consequently, the value of the company's shares? Is the Board appointing appropriate new executive directors? Should the roles of Chairman and Chief Executive be vested in one person or in two?

Who can answer these questions from the close knowledge of a company's affairs, and of the people involved, except a strong team of independent, non-executive directors? I firmly believe that the independent director is absolutely central to good corporate governance – not just as a safeguard for investors, but as a way of maximizing the company's potential.

My own experience has convinced me of the importance of this role. I was one of the five non-executive directors appointed to Guinness during the difficult days of 1986. And I am certain that the efforts of that team effectively saved the company. Certainly, its future would have been most uncertain had we not done what we did – and today Guinness is successful, profitable and truly one of the world's outstanding companies.

At Tesco, we have had independent directors for many years. They contribute, in an extremely positive way, to broad company strategy and chair our remuneration and audit committees. They keep a close eye on the activities of the Board, and help our executive directors to perform at their maximum potential. We have an independent Deputy Chairman who, among other duties, monitors my own activities as Chairman. All this is accepted by myself and by the Tesco Board as entirely healthy, constructive and very much to the good of the company, its employees and its shareholders.

So I see independent non-executive directors as the linchpin of good corporate governance. I believe they are extremely important; but they must be first-class people, genuinely independent and genuinely effective. It is not a role for the Chairman's friends and relatives, nor for people who lack relevant experience and ability. Because sometimes, if things look like going wrong, their role becomes both very taxing and vitally important to the future of the company and to the interests of investors.

And, when things are going well, the independent directors can provide invaluable strategic guidance and advice from their own experience in other, often quite dissimilar, organizations.

So I commend the *The Independent Director* in the hope that it will encourage more companies to recruit the right team of non-executive directors, and also lead to an increase in the numbers of experienced and successful businessmen and women who are willing to offer themselves for this most valuable role.

Sir Ian MacLaurin
Chairman, Tesco PLC

Preface

Directors are there to run a company on behalf of the share-holders; to be effective, they must be able to plan and implement strategy for increasing the return to shareholders without putting the company at financial risk. The presence of independent directors transforms a group of executives into a balanced board capable of properly handling the often conflicting pressures and interests of the various parties.

Independent directors are primarily valued for their objective judgement of corporate affairs. They may have a specific skill which can be exercised from time to time but, for the most part, their contribution will be rated by their overall knowledge and wisdom.

Judgement cannot be learned from reading a book – neither can wisdom. The best hope for anyone wishing to become an independent director is to develop his own judgement by exposing and testing his knowledge and experience in many different situations and learning from a wide cross-section of individuals.

An independent director, although legally bearing the same responsibilities as the executive directors, does not achieve effectiveness by controlling operations but by influencing decisions. This may be done in a number of ways depending upon the size of the company:

- The chairman or chief executive can often benefit from consulting an independent confidante before making important policy or executive decisions.
- The increasing use of board audit and remuneration sub-committees gives independent directors an opportunity to question and monitor important areas of executive competence, prudence and reward.
- An independent director should be able to question executive assumptions and decisions either from direct or indirect experience or because something 'does not smell right'. This should provide valuable insights into strategic thinking.
- Experienced independent directors will have their own methods of judging executive effectiveness. As monthly accounts only show problems several weeks after they have occurred, independent directors often have their own leading indicators for assessing how well the company is performing. It is no use 'staring at the wake to learn where the ship is going'.
- Independent directors may have specific areas of expertise not directly available to the executives. This can apply in many areas, professional, industrial, market or geographic.
- There may be times when independent directors have to prove their effectiveness by challenging the competence or honesty of the chairman or their executive colleagues, perhaps leading to dismissals.
- Ultimately, the most extreme action that can be taken by an independent director is resignation, so sending a signal to the shareholders or bankers that there is board conflict. Leaving a board should only be the last resort when all other action has failed.

The field of independent directorship is in no way a riskless pasture; it should not be entered lightly. It carries significant exposures, of financial liability, possible disqualification, and consequential damage to future careers.

A newcomer to the role, perhaps a rising executive in a major group, is well advised to study carefully the current status of the company and the prognosis. If things go wrong, he is exposed with the rest of the board, and he may be faced with the need to change senior officers, which is not the best introduction to the field.

For example, caution would be advisable with a company showing some of the following:

- Sales have been rising steeply from a number of acquisitions but profit margins and cash flow have been declining.
- Debt has been increasing while other balance sheet ratios have been deteriorating.
- Board salaries have risen steeply.
- There are three 'independent directors'. One is the recently retired chief executive and the two others are a local accountant and lawyer.
- The chairman is unfailingly optimistic that the diversification from recently acquired acquisitions will project the company on a new growth track.
- The company is shortly to seek a rights issue to strengthen the balance sheet and the financial advisers have recommended the appointment of another outside director.

Any one of these is a potentially hazardous situation for an incoming independent director. He might be well advised to decline the invitation unless he is expert in such situations, and goes in as the nominee of the majority shareholders or with powers from the leading bank.

One of the key requirements for effectiveness in the role is for the candidate to understand what he is entering, and to have done his homework thoroughly. Without it, he is likely to be ineffective and may well be at significant risk.

By the autumn of 1991 SYSPAS Ltd, a bureau specializing in company performance, reported that 23% of all UK listed industrial and distribution companies were at risk of financial stress; among these businesses 12 had sales in excess of £1bn and 47 had turnovers between £100m and £1bn. Moreover, of the 200 businesses in this category, 30 had the maximum risk ratings implying that there was an excellent chance of either failure or having to undergo major surgery in the near future.

This broad picture was supported when ICC Ltd, another bureau specializing in credit ratings and company comparisons, reported that in the third quarter of 1991 there were 64 companies (over 20% with sales in excess of £50m) which shared a common characteristic; they had a margin on sales of less than 5%, a current ratio of less than one and borrowings greater than 80% of shareholders' funds. In addition, around 40% of the boards (presumably with shareholders' agreement) had voted themselves large pay rises for their outstanding management performance.

Furthermore, an autumn 1991 survey of 268 independent directors from listed companies by Merton Associates (see References) showed nearly 60% of respondents reported that:

- They felt marginalized by the poor quality of briefings from the chairman or chief executive.
- The chairman did not heed objective advice.
- They were underutilized by the chairman.

While the survey does not correlate poor performance with a dismissive attitude to independent directors, it is likely that the quality of board decisions can only be adversely affected if those outside the executive group are not fully consulted.

The situation revealed by these three sources, raises the issue whether boards are performing as well as they might, and seriously questions whether independent directors are contributing as effectively as they could.

It is the principal purpose of this book to respond to these issues. The authoritative opinions reported demonstrate clearly the key importance of the chairman role in mobilizing or suppressing the skills and wisdom of the independent directors. They also indicate how best the independent director can make his contribution effective.

The contributors to this book are all individuals who have demonstrated their success as board members in a wide variety of situations. We as editors are indebted to them for the time and attention they have given and hope that their experience will encourage effectiveness both from chairmen and executives working with their colleagues and from independent directors themselves.

The results are presented in three Parts in this book:

Part One (Chapters 1–3) sets the background against which independent directors operate.
Part Two (Chapters 4–11) presents information directly relevant to potential or actual independent directors, chairmen and executive directors in performing and utilizing the role.

Part Three (Chapters 12–17) sets out the views of top authorities and their expectations of the role.

The structure is designed to permit convenient reading of individual chapters, as well as providing a rounded picture of the whole.

Throughout this book, a director is referred as 'he' rather than 'he or she' for the sake of brevity and convenience, despite the undoubted fact that there are a growing number of highly competent and well-qualified women being appointed to boards. It is hoped this book will prove equally useful to both sexes, and will help their particular skills and abilities to be used to the full.

William Houston
Nigel Lewis

Acknowledgements

We thank the many people who have kindly given time and attention to assisting in the preparation of this book. We have made every effort to reflect contributors' views, but errors are entirely ours. In particular, we wish to record our gratitude to the following: David Allen; Sir John Banham; Eric Barton; Peter Benton; Sir Adrian Cadbury; James Chalmers; Jonathan Charkham; Ron Clark; David Clarke; Sir John Collyear; Paul Daniels; David Darke; Peter Davis; Patrick Dunne; John Faris; Jon Foulds; Tina George; Clive Gilchrist; John Gillum; Richard Hargreaves; Sir John Harvey-Jones; Harry Hemens; Mark Homan; Colin Hope; Blenyth Jenkins; Rob Johnson; Michael Jordan; John Kinder; Gary Lefevre; Ian McDonald; Sir Ian MacLaurin; Alan McLintock; Peter Moody; Harold Mourgue; Hugh Parker; Brian Pearse; Giles Pitman; Sir David Plastow; Michael Queen; John Reeve; Richard Regan; Bruce Rhodes; David Russell; Anthony Ross; Frank Ruhemann; Derek Sach; Colin St Johnston; Michael Sandland; Andrew Soundy; Alan Spiers; Richard Taffler; Leslie Thomas; John Thomson; Sir John Trelawny; David Turle; Peter Waine; Sir Peter Walters; Sir Max Williams; Francis de Zulueta.

We would also like to thank Chris Woodward and his team in 3i's Marketing Department for making their facilities available to us during the preparation of this book. In particular, we thank the following for their patience, help and encouragement: Chris Woodward; Gail Croston; Matthew Kearney; Karen Kay; Carol Brennan; Sandra Byrne; Esther Tebrook; Tina Culling and Mike Sheard.

Finally, additional organizations from which key contributors gained much of their insight include: Advent; Barclays Bank; Baronsmead; BIM; BP; BT; BVCA; Cadbury Schweppes; CBI; Coopers & Lybrand Deloitte; Cork Gully; Gallaghers; GrandMet; Halifax Building Society; ICI; IOD; LBS; McKinsey; Midland Bank; NatWest Bank; NM Rothschild; Norwich Union; Plessey; Price Waterhouse; Pro Ned; Reed International; Rolls Royce; Special Risk Services; Sun Life; Tesco; Thames TV; TI; VESL; Vickers; Woolwich Building Society.

Part One

BACKGROUND TO THE ROLE

1

Becoming an independent director

Some time ago it was relatively easy to become a non-executive or independent director if you were a senior politician, a retired admiral or general or had a title. The work was not onerous. It meant turning up once a month, nodding agreement and then enjoying a good lunch, all for some 500 guineas a year.

The proportion of outside directors varied with the business. Banks used to have huge boards with only the chief executive belonging to the management team. Industrial companies tended to have no truly independent directors, many of the executive directors just stayed on the board as non-executives. Retired audit partners could enjoy a similar addition to their pensions.

During the 1970s there was a more general interest in board composition – probably because a number of fringe banks and conglomerates collapsed spectacularly. There were several reports included in the Bullock Inquiry on Industrial Democracy in 1977 which showed that out of 982 companies analysed (over 80% with 1000 or more employees), about 25% had no independent directors and nearly 40% had only one or two independent directors.

The next wave of failures in the early 1980s triggered a much more significant initiative with the creation of Pro Ned, an organization dedicated to researching and promoting the role of non-executive or independent directors. The first managing director was Jonathan Charkham from the Bank of England and the initiative was supported by the Council of the Stock Exchange, the DTI, CBI, BIM, the major banks, and institutions. By 1985, the initiative was having some success when the Bank of England Bulletin reported a survey showing that the number of listed company boards with no outsiders had declined to 6% and those with one or two was now over 30%.

In the early 1990s, the proportion of independent directors continues to increase. The tradition for financially based companies to have a majority of independent directors has continued while many industrially based companies are seeking parity between executive and independent directors. This process has been greatly encouraged by the banks and institutions who want to see a greater degree of control exercised over charismatic entrepreneurs, such as those who dominated many of the 1980 star performing companies.

Independence

The terms 'non-executive director', 'outside director', and 'independent director' are often used more or less interchangeably. The former is in wide use but has perhaps a somewhat negative flavour; the second is common in the USA; and the latter is used increasingly, mainly because the idea of independence is generally (but not always) fundamental to the nature of the role. Such directors should generally be independent in these senses:

- They should not have been an executive of the company within the last few years.
- They should not have recently acted as a professional adviser to the company.
- There should not be a trading relationship either as a supplier or customer.
- They should not be financially dependent upon the company.
- Directors should be independent of the chairman and other directors, executive and non-executive.

- They should not be rewarded by share options or bonus schemes. There may be some exceptions where a company doctor is brought in to rescue the company.
- However, they should be sufficiently rewarded to attract people of stature who will take the trouble to learn about the company and make a contribution.

Making the appointment

The chairman normally makes board appointments advised by other board members, and these are later ratified by the shareholders. Ideally he should be wholly objective in assessing the needs of the business and then recommending skills for balancing board talents. Unfortunately, Pro Ned reported in 1991 that only 10% of independent board appointments for PLCs were made through agencies; while it is quite usual for very senior people to be known by reputation, it is likely that many appointments are still made from too small a circle through close links with the chairman.

Maximizing the contribution

Impact depends partly upon the individual and partly on the rest of the board, particularly the chairman.

The involvement of the individual

He must be prepared to involve himself and learn the business. In the 1970s it was common for independent directors to glance through board papers on the way to a meeting and remind themselves of the 'perceptive' questions they wanted to ask. This is no longer tolerated on most boards, each director is required to understand the business and make a contribution.

In smaller companies many directors are chosen for a specific skill to complement executive talents. In larger companies and PLCs independent directors are more likely to be chosen for their wider business judgement and for their competence to serve on audit, remuneration or other committees.

In the freewheeling days of the 1980s many directors felt that they had little function other than supporting the executives. This perception has changed in the early 1990s. If things go wrong, the banks and institutions will expect the independent directors to play a significant part in implementing remedial measures.

The board environment

Independent directors are only as good as the chairman will allow them to be. It is fruitless for a competent person to join a badly run board – that is unless they have the proxy vote of a large block of shares. It says little for an individual's reputation and judgement if he accepts a directorship only to discover the board's work is paralysed and he has to resign.

Reasons for an appointment

From the candidate's standpoint: the fees are seldom a significant attraction, but there can be strong reasons if one can identify with the aims and future of the business.

From the company's standpoint: to give a board the balance which changes it from an all-executive management meeting into a leavened group equipped to handle the often conflicting pressures and interests of the various parties. The presence of independent directors requires the executive directors to take account of their colleagues' views, experience and knowledge. These are some of the ways in which the executives can use independent directors:

- Helping formulate strategy that reflects a wider business awareness.
- Advising how best to achieve a management structure that is manned by competent people able to implement the board's policy. They should also ensure that there is suitable management succession and that the pay structure reflects the responsibilities and performance of the business.
- Monitoring performance of the company against budgets and plans.
- Demonstrating to those outside the business that the company is

managed with integrity and efficiency. Specialized sub-committees are being increasingly used to improve board effectiveness by predigesting routine business and monitoring performance.

- Helping determine the priorities for board discussion and the agenda headings.
- In extremis, taking control of the business in cases of fraud or incompetence. This might mean running the company until new executives can be appointed.

Judging effectiveness

In judging the effectiveness of an independent director, much depends upon the size of the business and the required role of the individual. For example, a venture capital chairman or chief executive may require a confidante with whom he can mull over a new idea. The position may be different for the chief executive of a large PLC seeking counsel whether to make a major acquisition or enter a new market.

Assuming that the board accepts the principle of having independent director(s), an individual's effectiveness can generally be judged on:

- Sound objective business judgement and commercial nous.
- Capacity to deliver his views with authority.
- Ability to pick up an unfamiliar brief rapidly.
- Feel for how to present his views in a manner acceptable to his colleagues.
- Ability to weigh others' arguments even though they differ from his own.
- Sense when a situation does not 'smell right' and the ability to persuade others of the concern.
- The fortitude to hold an opinion or carry through a correct course of action even though it might mean unpopularity or being voted off the board.

Interest in these and other aspects of the independent director's role are increasing steadily. The aim of this book is to draw together and present the experience and views of a wide range of top practitioners connected with this field.

2

How the board works

One fundamental difference between a board and a management meeting is the presence of independent directors who are not responsible to the chief executive. They are there to form a critical mass which should ensure that the executives responsible for tactical control of a business are obliged to take into account the strategic long-term future and to weigh the sometimes conflicting interests of the various parties.

The board is the top decision-making body of an enterprise, it is appointed by the shareholders and is accountable to them for the company's progress and continuity. The board is composed of directors whose first responsibility is to the company as an entity, then to the shareholders as a whole.

An example of this particular conflict occurred in 1990. An important unit trust group stated their priority as shareholders was for companies to maintain dividend continuity even though the directors placed greater emphasis on cash flow during the recession. If enough shareholders held the same views as the unit trust their collective remedy was to call an emergency general meeting (EGM), remove the board and try to appoint one following their diktat.

In the majority of companies managers and shareholders are one and the same people who, not unreasonably, run the company for their own purposes. The position changes once the shareholders decide to introduce outside capital – perhaps from a venture capitalist who often insists on certain conditions, such as appointment of an outside independent director.

The workings of the board should likewise change with the stage of the company, though the broad features remain unchanged:

- The board is run by the chairman who is responsible for board agenda, conduct of meetings and the preparation of correct minutes. He has the responsibility for representing the company to the outside world.
- The board formulates corporate aims that are acceptable to a spread of shareholders who may not have common objectives. Some may be long-term investors who do not mind whether dividend payouts are subordinated to creating long-term cash flow; others may be short-term investors who wish to maximize their return.
- It ensures that a sound future strategy and plan is established to manage the business in line with these aims.
- It watches out for early warning of changing business conditions or competitive pressures that may require changes to the plan.
- It ensures that the company has resources, particularly money and people, sufficient and capable of implementing the strategy.
- It ensures that financial systems are accurate, timely, will deter possible fraud, and represent assets at their correct value.
- It monitors performance against the plan, and takes corrective action if necessary.
- As well as its prime obligation to the company and trusteeship for shareholders, the board fulfils its obligations towards employees, customers, suppliers and the community.

How these are fulfilled

The ideal solution is to have a chairman who can lead the company at any stage of its growth. Styles can change. There are companies such as Hanson, Amstrad and Racal whose chairmen have taken their companies through flotation to be major forces; others have outgrown their creator who has wisely ceded the role to another or had to be replaced.

- First and foremost the chairman should be a leader of the whole, while the chief executive or managing director (in UK usage) is responsible for day-to-day operations. The institutions like to see these posts separated as the two individuals have their own distinctive roles and duties. However, the most effective companies are often led by individuals combining both roles.
- It is unusual for a non-executive (or more aptly, part-time) chairman to have a staff of his own. He should work with the company secretary, chief executive and finance director to ensure that the board agenda is correctly balanced and that all documents are available for directors in good time for the board meeting. He should also ensure that proposals are adequately thought through and presented to enable the board to arrive at a decision.
- The chairman should ensure the board has a clear sense of mission and objectives. These might for example, entail technological leadership, market share, return on capital, earnings per share growth or overseas expansion.
- To be effective, the board should have a balance of suitably qualified and experienced people of comparable force and dominance. It is primarily the task of the chairman to see that the board is made up of such individuals, which many authorities consider should number between nine and 15 people.
- The board should also be efficient. Part of the chairman's task is to see that the best possible decisions are reached in the time available through an agenda which balances forward thinking and monitoring present performance. The time available can be used more efficiently if issues have been previously digested through judicious use of sub-committees.
- The board's composition should be changed through rotation to meet the changing strategy and according to economic circumstances. This can be achieved through fixed-term appointments which the chairman can implement without unduly upsetting existing directors.

Board Committees

Harold Mougue. Independent director and Audit Committee Chairman

Harold Mougue is a director of N M Rothschild and serves on the boards as an independent director of T & N, Rolls Royce, Thames Television and Nuswift; he is also chairman of Kenwood. He serves on the audit committee of all these companies some as chairman.

Mougue is no stranger to financial and cost accounts having served at one time as a finance director of an industrial company. He sees the audit committee as an independent check on the financial system where there is complete openness between the committee, the auditors and the financial department. Although the audit committee meets formally twice a year before the interim and preliminary results are released to the board, there is constant communication with the financial director both at and outside board meetings. Overall, he estimates that committee service occupies 3.5 days/year for each company.

An audit committee relies heavily on auditors for detailed feedback to assess any deficiencies or shortcomings in the financial systems. Their evaluation is critical. In a number of recent failures, the committee has been given either incorrect or incomplete information which has contributed significantly to the companies' downfall. Mougue believes that the committee can only work successfully when it has the full support of the chairman to deal with such matters as firing the finance director or a change of auditors.

It is essential that each member of an audit committee has a sufficient understanding of the business to enable them to focus on essential matters. The task is somewhat complicated for a non-technical person in a company like Rolls Royce or in a contracting business which could receive a major claim. In every case, chairmen should ensure that there is sufficient industry knowledge to forewarn the board to make provisions when needed.

Independent directors who also sit on the finance committee should also have their own leading indicators to judge a company's progress and to be aware where dangers may arise. Mougue points out that too short a term as an independent director can lead to an incomplete understanding of executive competence. For example, recurring problems inevitably seem to come from the same source and one learns to place more or less reliability on the individual concerned.

The American practice of audit, remuneration and other committees has now been adopted by most listed companies in Britain. Detailed practices vary:

- Audit committees are designed to give the independent directors confidential access to the auditors with (usually) the chief executive and finance director attending by invitation. The group meets three to four times a year and considers:

  – The review of the financial statements before publication.
  – Any irregularities or shortcomings that should be reported to the board.
  – The adequacy of the internal systems.
  – Whether the present auditors should be re-appointed and the scale of their fees.

- The remuneration committee (also sometimes called the chairman's committee) normally consists entirely of independent directors. It meets three to four times a year to discuss the remuneration and benefit packages of the executive directors and senior managers. It may also consider executive promotion or dismissal and be concerned with management succession.

Other groups have been established to meet the particular needs of different business:

- The special circumstances of building societies make it advantageous for the Halifax to have a treasury committee.
- Where a financial services group has to comply with the financial services act, it is usual to have a compliance committee (which may be combined with the audit committee).
- Where there is a combined chairman and chief executive it is usual to have a non-executive committee chaired by a senior independent director. It should monitor performance and can recommend removal of the chairman or chief executive.
- Some boards have accounts committees whose job is to 'look behind' the board statements and require further information to be reported if this is necessary.
- It is not unusual for boards to have a strategy committee comprising executive and independent directors depending on the group structure. It is designed to combine the 'top-down'

approach of the independent directors with the bottom-up view of the executives.

Board composition

Britain and the USA companies have both a unitary board (where every director has an equal responsibility), an arrangement favoured over the two-tier board used in Germany. The board varies depending on the type of business. American boards and financial companies usually have a majority of independent directors. This proportion has not been followed by UK industrial companies which usually have two executives to every one independent director, although the proportions are changing. This is how a number of chairmen have expressed their ideas of the independent director contribution. The independent director should:

- Not depend upon the company for their means of livelihood.
- Be responsible for directing but not managing the business. Most chairman want their independent directors to understand the company's business – but view it from the outside.
- Contribute to work of the company through the committee structure.
- Monitor, and if necessary fire, the executives. Some groups go further, the Delta Group look upon independent directors as the company's 'external examiners'.
- Be appointed for a three-year term which can be renewed by agreement with the chairman, though some suggest that five years should be a minimum. Rotation is a good way of culling board members if different skills are needed.
- Be prepared to assume executive responsibilities if things go wrong. Fortunately it is rare for independent directors, with or without shareholder or bank support, to have to remove the chairman or chief executive for incompetence or alleged wrong-doing.

The composition varies depending upon the type of business:

- A company heavily involved in property such as a building society or retail chain will generally have a chartered surveyor.
- It is usual to have an independent director with a background of finance to act as a foil and to support the finance director.
- There might well be a lawyer on the board of a financial services company.
- A company relying on technical development may have a senior academic in the particular discipline.
- Most boards of whatever size like to include a senior industrialist.
- A company wishing to enter a new market such as the USA or Japan may wish to have a national of that country to advise on the business culture – not principally to introduce new business.
- Companies sensitive to the working of Westminster or Whitehall have found it useful to have on the board a politician or a civil servant on secondment.
- The Company's circumstances can also affect the choice:

  > The composition should vary with time. In good times, the board should include a full-blown entrepreneur. When approaching a recession it would be wise to recruit a good defensive player.
  >
  > When times are hard and fast moving, some companies like to have a thoroughly 'streetwise' individual on the board.

Board styles change with business cycles.

Business cycles have a impact on strategy depending upon the operating time scale. For example:

- Heavily research-orientated companies with a long lead time may be less affected by a recession. Expenditure will depend more on balance sheet strength than economic conditions.
- Conversely a company heavily dependent upon growth through acquisition will need to reduce debt and become cash rich before a recession. They can then pick up assets cheaply when prices fall.

The board's public face

Board styles vary considerably depending upon the stature, knowledge and personality of the individuals around the board table. This reflects on the conduct of board meetings but also on the outside world of shareholders, bankers, the local community etc.

It is normal in a listed company for the chairman and chief executive to be aware of the need to communicate. Chairman of companies supported by venture capital may not give the same priority to communication but independent directors should encourage those concerned to show a public face. These are some of the occasions when a board should be aware of its external responsibilities:

- The chairman and chief executive should make themselves available to shareholders for explaining the work of the board, its aims and objectives and strategy for achieving results.
- It is also important to keep closely in touch with the lenders particularly if there is a lead bank. Relations are particularly important if the company is in danger of breaching the bank covenants.
- Public relations has a key role in positioning the company for implementing strategy. There are many examples of both defensive and offensive policy options.

What happens if things go wrong?

Companies generally go wrong not through bad luck but bad management. There are two major causes:

- They have misjudged the impact of the business cycle.
- The board has made a commercial misjudgment which it has failed to rectify. Many commercial mistakes are to do with acquisitions that the board has neither the understanding nor the competence to manage.

Spotting misjudgments

Cognoscenti of company reports and accounts will be aware of the occasions when the chairman's statement and the financial statements diverge. The chairman's report hails continuing success; the financial accounts show rising sales, reducing margins, rising debt and small but frequent asset write-downs.

From inside the company the position should be more evident. For example:

- The board papers become less and less informative. The *Company Chairman* by Sir Adrian Cadbury (see References) cites the case of Professor Louis Cabot who went on the board of Penn Central Railroad a few months before it crashed. Cabot reports that at each board meeting, which lasted only 90 minutes, the board was invited to discuss a long list of small capital expenditure items without addressing the real issues; searching questions were fobbed off by the executive's unfailing optimism. The professor's letter of complaint coincided with the final collapse.
- Outside directors should be as much aware of board paper omissions as inclusions. De Lorean directors should have been alerted to the problems in the company when financial information presented to the board was either incomplete or on scraps of paper.
- Losses are reported quite properly in the accounts and the balance sheet shows a continuous deterioration but the executive directors have no remedial plans. The chairman tries to protect the executives by curtailing discussion while expressing continuing optimism.

What should be done

Even if the company is not in immediate danger of financial distress the non-executives have a clear duty to the company and to the shareholders. Their task is to recognize dangerous symptoms of decline then take action together if this is possible, or singly if necessary.

These are some of the circumstances that might arise:

- The chairman is not capable of directing or controlling a headstrong chief executive who refuses to admit his mistakes. If after an informal approach by the independent directors the chairman refuses to take action, they should officially require the chairman to resign. If they cannot obtain a majority around the board table, they should minute their disapproval and approach the institutional shareholders.
- Non-executive directors can (and should) require the removal of a venal, bumbling or incompetent chairman if they can secure board majority.
- Independent directors are deemed to be aware if their company is trading wrongfully. Their first duty is to require the executives to take remedial action. If their combined approach still cannot move the executives they should minute their concern and inform the rest of the board that they reserve the right to approach the shareholders and the lead bank. If all else fails, it is their duty to resign.
- The institutional investment committees or institutions working together can initiate the removal of the chairman and/or chief executive after a series of poor results.
- The chief executive is either incompetent or is misinforming the board. The chairman and the independent directors should be able to terminate his contract and those of other directors also likely to be involved. Depending upon the Articles of Association, it is usual for the board to be able to remove a director with a 75% majority.

The penalties for board incompetence

Under Common Law a director is in a position of trust towards the company, should act in its best interest and should exercise whatever skill he may have with reasonable care.

The 1986 Insolvency Act places additional requirements on all directors above the Common Law requirements. These are tough. A director may be deemed personally liable if the company is accused of trading fraudulently or of wrongful trading. This is a new penalty which is still being tested in the courts. These are the tests to be applied if the liquidator is to prove wrongful trading:

- The company's assets are not sufficient to meet its debts, other liabilities and the costs of liquidation.
- At some time before winding up the director knew, or ought to have concluded, that there was no reasonable prospect of the company avoiding insolvent liquidation.
- He was, or had been a director for up to two years before insolvency proceedings.
- The court is satisfied that the director did not take 'every step' he ought to have taken to minimize the potential loss to creditors.

The Insolvency Court will consider:

- The general knowledge, skill and experience that might reasonably be expected of someone carrying out the role of director.
- The general skill and experience actually possessed by the individual.

To fulfil the requirements of the Act, a director is now required to:

- Recognize when the company can no longer avoid insolvent liquidation.
- Take immediate and positive action to protect the interests of creditors.
- Possess the skills appropriate to his function and be expected to use them.

The penalties for conviction of fraudulent or wrongful trading are serious. Those found guilty might be:

- Required to pay a contribution to the assets for settlement with the creditors and liquidator.
- Disqualified from serving as a director for a period from two to 15 years.

While such situations can and do occur and can give rise to serious consequences, in practice, the great majority of companies, boards and directors never experience them at first hand.

3

Contrasting roles in large and small companies

The role of an independent director alters as a company develops from the start-up stage through various points of change until it is a mature PLC. The types of task and problem faced by board and management vary considerably. Nevertheless, certain qualities are always needed in an independent director: these include broad business experience; ability to assess and to handle people; strength to hold one's ground; financial numeracy; awareness of the legal environment and obligations to the various parties; familiarity with board practice; and the ability to act as the chairman's sounding board.

In addition, there is often a need for the independent director to have experience of an industry akin to that of the company. This often applies to smaller companies, for example, a consumer goods specialist might not be welcomed with open arms to the board of a small software company. Despite this, there are situations where the specific need is to add a completely new perspective.

In general, the prime requirements depend critically on the stage or category of the company. In order to examine this evolving picture, it is helpful to classify companies into the following categories: start-up, management buy-out/management buy-in (MBO/MBI), family company, organic growth, acquisition growth, flotation, quoted company, and rescue/turnround. These categories are not mutually exclusive, but typify common stages or points of change in the life of a company, some of which may on occasion coincide with fund-raising.

The rest of this chapter considers the specific requirements of executive directors, and particularly of independent directors for each of these categories. Much of the following material was contributed by Michael Queen, Anthony Ross and Eric Barton of 3i.

Start-up

Situation

A relatively inexperienced management team forms the core of an immature board, but has good knowledge of products, markets and production. Often there is recognition of the need for financial skills, and these may be provided part or full-time, and may or may not be represented on the board. Sales start from a low level, and the cash forecast depends critically on the top line.

Executive directors

The key tasks for the executive directors are to build up the human and financial resources to achieve monthly cash breakeven within the aggregate funding available. This demands a wide range of skills, industry and market knowledge, energy, motivating others, judgement, and a subtle blend of overoptimism and realism.

Independent directors

The independent director's role is to act as an experienced sounding board, comforter, and challenger to the managing director/chairman. In a start-up the priorities will usually be cash management and sales/marketing.

At times, the independent director may need to weigh in and work hands-on beside the executives, perhaps to seek extra funding, or to help find an extra sale. He may be called upon to unravel confused working relationships, or lines of responsibility, or perhaps to remind the board that they are in danger of trading wrongfully.

Frequently the independent director is the only one with experience of board work and practice, with an awareness of the differing perspectives of shareholders and management, and dealing with external sources of finance.

An incoming independent director sponsored by 'new money' is not usually welcomed at first by an experienced board. The feeling is that his presence is a costly intrusion which can only be justified if it also brings sales contacts. The perspective changes if the independent director can smooth the company's passage through tough or difficult water.

Management buy-out/management buy-in

Situation

In both cases, an experienced operating management will have departed from its corporate umbrella, and for the first time faces the tasks of running an independent company with all its obligations to outside shareholders and banks. The MBO situation somewhat resembles a start-up, while a MBI has the benefit of an experienced incoming shareholder/chief executive. In both cases, however, significant sales may be flowing from the outset, but this advantage is partly offset by high borrowings and consequently, a stretched revenue position. This problem is only likely to be resolved by a steady flow of retained profits, or by unwinding capital or current assets or a saleable business activity. It follows that the prospects for a business in this stage are particularly closely linked to timing in the business cycle.

Executive directors

The executives have to hold the act together, exploit the one-off opportunity to raise motivation and efficiency, and above all, keep close to the task of degearing. Unless cash is generated all will fail.

Independent directors

The role of the independent director is similar to that in a start-up, except that cash generation is more important than winning sales. A good independent director will add business nous to executives – knowledgeable about their industry but short of general experience.

Family company

Situation

Family businesses generally have stable board and management structures, which is both their strength and their weakness. If the team is competent, the clarity and confidence of the company can lead to impressive and enduring performance. On the other hand, it is not uncommon for such teams to become introverted and blindly satisfied with how matters are run, despite the emergence of new threats or opportunities.

Shareholdings may be spread among numerous relatives and generations, and some relations may be directors. This mixture of roles and relationships can sometimes make for a confused picture that demands high skills in handling personal relationships, for example in dealing with the major tensions that can arise from diverging aspirations.

Executive directors

The main task is to keep an outward-looking posture, so as to develop the business based on a stable shareholder register. This may entail handling an awkward set of relationships (and some-times relations) externally and sometimes internally, as the executive directors may often be family members.

Independent directors

The key responsibility is to give a (possibly) inward looking board a sense of reality, and an encouragement to grasp new opportunities. The independent director needs to achieve the difficult balancing act of simultaneously pushing the company forward in the changing world, and smoothing and maintaining satisfactory family relationships. This task can be extremely taxing, but equally rewarding.

Organic growth

Situation

Organic growth is the natural state of a start-up or MBO and features heavily in the history of such majors as IBM and Sainsburys. The pressures arise from the growth rate. Low rates of 10% per year impose no special pressures, but if these rise to 100% per year, 'stability' comes to mean perpetual flux. Companies such as Amstrad and many silicon valley companies have seen such rates of change. Life in this environment is something very remote from normal business experience, and in many ways it is closer to the start-up entrepreneur's first year.

Executive directors

The main problem is to maintain the intense rate of growth, and contain the sense of instability (and sometimes insecurity) that can accompany it. It is a matter of reconciling the flexibility essential to permit the changes, with the structure needed for financial and quality control. It calls for rare skills, but has the helpful feature that companies in this stage are exciting and fun to work for. Maintaining the right formula over time is not easy; perhaps Hewlett Packard is one company that has come closer than most.

Independent directors

The independent directors may face the classic problem of a board with an entrepreneurial chief executive, who has a strong vision, and is often disinclined to listen to contrary opinions. In extreme cases, this can present real difficulties that can only be resolved if there is more than one independent director. The dilemma is that often such executives have the vision and the drive; yet they may have to be restrained or removed if they are not to lead the company over a precipice. The key skill is therefore the ability to handle this relationship so as to reconcile these considerations, and to promote the growth without sacrificing control.

Rapid growth makes substantial demands on the board and management in changing the processes, systems, people, hierarchies, organization and financial arrangements. This attaches particular value to an independent director who has often seen the task of managing the process of change at first hand before.

Acquisition growth

Situation

The company has determined to follow a policy of growth through acquisition. At best, this is part of a well-thought-out strategy, which may involve shifting the whole product/market posture of the company – for example like TI; or a company may have a dealing strategy such as Hanson; or a sector blanketing strategy such as ICI's policy for paints. Others follow diversification for less sound reasons, for example as a defensive move when the company is already under pressure in its existing markets. The danger is that the anticipated benefits often turn out to be elusive.

Executive directors

Realism and competence are the key requirements. Acquisition is often seen as the escape route from a tight corner, yet the evidence is that a high proportion of mergers are judged in retrospect to have been disappointing or failures. On the other hand, companies with the right skills have repeated successes. Other important factors are the degree of integration with the existing business, and the quantum of central oversight/control. These factors determine where synergy enters the picture if at all.

The financial dimension is fundamental: balance sheet shape, anticipated profits and EPS growth. At boom periods in the cycle, there is a temptation to show attractive progress highly geared through acquisitions or repeated use of overrated paper.

Independent directors

In many respects, the needs are similar to those for organic growth, though the corporate finance dimension is often more prominent. The independent directors need to apply a cautious restraining influence, particularly where an acquisition is seen at the board table as an escape route. First-hand experience of having lived through mergers and their aftermath, are invaluable to such a board.

Flotation

Situation

The company is established as a profit generator and the shares are judged fit to offer to a wider market. The present board with shareholder backing has decided that this is the route it wishes to follow.

Executive directors

Executive responsibilities fall under two heads. First, the company must be managed to standards appropriate for a public company, so the executives must ensure that suitable systems are in place. Second, they must ensure that the company follows the regulations that apply to listed companies, and to the process of becoming listed.

Independent directors

Independent directors have much to contribute if they have previously served on the board of another flotation. They should also bring substantial experience of PLC board work. If this experience is lacking in the executives, it is essential it lies with the independent directors.

Board composition is an important aspect of preparing a company for flotation, and it is the chairman's task to ensure that this is appropriately handled.

Quoted company

Situation

This ranges from a recently floated USM company to the largest listed multinational.

Executive directors

The executives are responsible for running the business within the plans and strategies that have been approved by the board. This should be in the best interests of company and shareholders as a body, and with due regard for the regulations surrounding the quoted company.

Independent directors

The independent director's main role is to ensure that the board has a strategy which is capable of implementation and then monitor performance. He also watches over the interests of the shareholders and other external parties in tune with the Company Acts and other legislation.

Independent directors may also be required to take the lead in acting if major problems become apparent. They play something of a watchdog role which contrasts with their guide/mentor role in, for example, a start-up.

Independent directors have also a major part to play in board governance by serving on committees, such as the Audit Committee and the Remuneration Committee. If an MBO should be proposed, the non-executive part of the board will often separate from the interested parties until the offer is resolved in one direction or the other; the non-executives represent the interests of the current shareholders, while some executives may act for their MBO team. This is usually seen as the best available, though far from ideal, way of protecting the shareholders' interests. It is recognized that the executives will inevitably have better knowledge of the company than anyone else.

It is important that independent directors understand that institutions may wish to change the board make-up through the company's life in order to introduce different skills.

Rescue/turnround

Situation

This is a common scenario. A company's net worth has been declining over several years and losses have been caused by uncorrected commercial mismanagement. If it is a public company, often the chairman's statement will be at variance with the reported figures, in the hope and belief that the problems will disappear. They seldom do.

Executive directors

The failure is almost always a failure of the executives, which has not been confronted and handled by the chairman and independent directors.

Independent directors

The independent directors are as much to blame in law as the other directors in the event of fraudulent or wrongful trading. However, there may be mitigating circumstances – if, for example, the board papers were themselves fraudulent. The penalties are serious and if guilty, a director may be fined or disqualified, or both.

The qualities particularly needed of the independent director, are the ability to read accurately the gravity and the possibilities of the company's position, and the courage to avoid being talked into a false perception of the realities. Specific skills include the ability to read the underlying value of a balance sheet, knowledge of the relevant law and the skill to bring the most effective pressure to bear for essential changes without having to use the nuclear weapon of resignation. Finally, how to minimize unnecessary personal exposures. When the company is in danger of wrongful or fraudulent trading the threat of resignation will not avoid personal liability along with other directors.

Part Two

THE ROLE IN PRACTICE

4

Independent director recruitment

There must be at least twice as many potential candidates seeking a non-executive directorship as there are vacancies. In the first place, the majority of openings are filled directly from personal knowledge of individuals, secondly there is still a reluctance – particularly in smaller companies – to see the need for an outsider. Furthermore, there is often a desire on both sides that the appointment will enhance his own standing.

From the individual's standpoint, it is essentially a marketing task to potential chairmen based on a sound track record. The person should already have good familiarity with board work, usually by working up the executive hierarchy of general management; it can also be gained by starting a business or as a successful professional adviser.

To sell himself, the individual can seek to join lists or registers such as those of Pro Ned or 3i that are described below, and make himself known to financial institutions and professional advisers. Regrettably, even in 1992, the majority of independent director appointments are still made through chairman contact (direct or indirect) and only gradually is the more professional approach gaining ground.

As a result, the individual should build on his contact network by coming to the attention of future chairman through merit either as an executive or in some professional role. There is no simple route to this; much depends on personal abilities, a flare for self-marketing and, perhaps, some luck!

As in marriage making, both parties are (in fact) seeking, consciously or unconsciously, a partner to flatter their self-image. This has the effect that claims are often heard that there are 'no good independent director candidates available' and 'there are no opportunities'. Both statements are untrue. The problem is that companies cannot always find what they feel they deserve and the opportunities are not easily visible to the individual. A side effect is that an individual generally has his greatest problem in finding his first few appointments; thereafter, he becomes more sought after.

However there is a change. In the last ten years the rapidly changing needs for boardroom skills have led chairmen to seek professional advice for the following:

- An assessment of the current strengths and weaknesses around the board table.
- The needs of the business.
- The qualities needed to achieve a balanced board.

This chapter describes the operations of four agencies working in the UK with examples of how they liaise with their clients.

Colin St Johnston, Director General of Pro Ned

Pro Ned was set up in 1982 by the Stock Exchange, the Bank of England and the institutions for the purpose of improving the quality of quoted company boards. It plays an active part in campaigning for the more effective use of independent directors as well as assisting their clients find the most suitable individuals. Although Pro Ned caters mostly for the needs of listed companies, it is also happy to act for smaller, privately owned companies who can gain as much from an independent director as larger concerns.

Pro Ned place around 100 individuals a year, estimated to represent only 10% of the total number appointed – the great majority being placed through direct contact. This may be a comfortable position for the chairman and perhaps executive directors but in Pro Ned's view, it may not be the best either for the company or its shareholders because the individual is unlikely to be truly independent.

Colin St Johnston emphasizes that independent directors are there to see that the board fulfils its first obligation to the shareholders as a whole; it then has responsibilities to other groups such as suppliers, customers, employees, and the local community. The independent director should also contribute to policy making and he has a duty to monitor the executives. To do this, he must make judgements about the organization and the quality of the executives.

In the main, chairmen of listed companies want an independent director who has served on a PLC main board, a consideration which excludes many otherwise potentially excellent candidates.

Clients have a wide choice from a register containing individuals who are still working full-time and others who are working independently perhaps having taken early retirement. Pro Ned believes the latter group has much to contribute, particularly in board debates on strategy. Here an independent director can be particularly helpful in playing back the outside view of a company's competitive position; it is sometimes difficult for executives to be wholly dispassionate about the pressures they face!

Board composition should reflect a balance of talents. For example independent directors might include an entrepreneur, someone who acts as a devil's advocate, possibly a financial man and another who might be particularly familiar with doing business in an important market – the whole providing a balanced view. Unlike choosing directors for a buy-out, it is generally not necessary to have industry skill on a larger company's board because that is provided by the executives.

An independent director should encourage the chairman and executives to establish close links with the shareholders and bankers, who will often be reassured by the presence of capable and known directors. An independent director should be able to speak about a company to a wide external constituency but not act as company spokesman unless particularly commissioned by the board. Executive board members should also be able to look to an independent director for suggestions about the company's contribution to local affairs, environmental issues and working within the community.

An independent director should make it his business to learn about the company and feed back his impressions to the executives. Among his roles are visiting the sites, meeting the people at all divisional levels, and walking the factory or office floor. He should see and be seen as being his own man, not just the chairman's crony. In addition to being visible he should also devote time and effort so as to be seen to be contributing. In particular, he should learn about the financial systems, the composition of board reports and what underlies the figures. He should also know what information should be coming to the directors and, even more significant what is not reported.

Ideally, a director should be appointed for an initial three-year period with the option of an additional three years if the relationship is working. Sometimes a chairman can be successfully promoted from among the independent directors which makes for a smooth transition from a tested relationship. However this is often impossible because the role of a part-time chairman typically requires one day per week. Probably for this reason, some 35% of all Pro Ned's assignments are for chairmen.

Making an appointment

The main source of Pro Ned shortlists is a data base of 700 individuals culled from 7,000 applications. Choice from the data base can be made under some 250 classifications: for example, there are over 20 different qualifications, 25 work specializations, 30 manufacturing classifications and a further 40 in the service sector. If no suitable candidate is found from the data base, a special search unit becomes involved. In 1991, the data base was being expanded by Pro Ned approaching individuals believed to be good independent director material. Ninety per cent of individuals on the register have had board experience on one of Britain's top 500 companies; each has been interviewed and references taken.

When an assignment is accepted, one of Pro Ned's directors visits the company, meets the chairman and chief executive and generally acquires a feel for the business by walking the premises. Pro Ned builds up a profile of the ideal candidate which is sent to the client for approval or amendment. Once this specification has been agreed it takes up to 30 days to produce a list of six to eight names from the data base – all of whom meet the specification and are known to be available. At this preliminary stage there is no disclosure of the client's name.

Once the client has narrowed the list to two candidates, the individuals are informed and are sent information on the company such as the report and accounts and brokers, circulars. They also receive details of the officers they will be meeting should they decide to proceed. The final choice is made by the company. Both sides have to be comfortable with each other, with the contribution sought and the time required. If, however, no candidate is acceptable then a further selection is made from the data base within the fee structure or, if that does not work, a search is undertaken.

An example

Paul Daniels, Chairman of S Daniels PLC

Before its flotation, Daniels' financial adviser, Robert Fleming, recommended that an independent director should be recruited. At the time this was resisted by the chairman but later in the 1980s an individual was introduced by the firm's stockbrokers who acted successfully as the chairman's sounding board on strategy and general corporate matters. Unfortunately, the individual could no longer continue because of illness and the chairman had to look elsewhere.

In his search, Paul Daniels was encouraged to attend a Pro Ned conference at which the speakers included Sir Adrian Cadbury and Hugh Parker. This proved a great success resulting in Colin St Johnston being asked to visit the company. Daniels was impressed by Pro Ned's appraisal and commissioned an assignment. Pro Ned interrogated their register, and produced seven names, from which Daniels decided to see three.

The individuals were rated by a personal evaluation on seven criteria leading to an aggregate possible score of 60. These were competence (out of 10), personal chemistry (out of 10), relevant experience (out of 10), age and location (out of 5), trustworthy (out of 5), will share our ambitions (out of 5), will contribute (out of 10), work hard (out of 5).

The candidates were sent corporate literature describing the business and the chairman saw each of the individuals for about 90 minutes; they later met the finance director for half an hour. When the right person is appointed, Daniels will look to him for wisdom and experience and contributions to strategy and longer term issues.

Peter Waine, Chief Executive of Hanson Green

The company started in 1974 operating under its previous name of Directorships Appointments Ltd. Peter Waine was an ex-CBI director who saw an opportunity for helping companies to recruit the right calibre of independent directors. Hanson Green specializes in small public companies, often located outside London. More recently demand has come from foreign firms setting up subsidiaries in the UK.

An independent director's first responsibility is clearly to the company as a whole but Peter Waine finds that most appointments are required as confidantes of the chairman and are always of main board calibre. For the most part, they are being recruited for their general ability, although more recently, individuals are also being sought with some specialized expertise. They may, for example, bring contacts, industry knowledge or specialist expertise; for example, one retailer wishing to expand sought an individual with a property development background; another might seek company doctoring skills. More recently people have been sought with knowledge of PR, marketing or particular countries in Europe.

Hanson Green begins with initial research, and then draws up a specification. This step is critically important and is fundamental to a successful assignment. The consultant should establish the level of the board's commitment to appointing a new independent director, what he is expected to contribute to the board, and the time required. Discussions will primarily be with the chairman and chief executive but will also include other independent directors.

Once the specification has been agreed a search is conducted for a potential short list using a data base of some 50 people that is continually updated and purged. Candidates vary widely in background and it is not always the most obvious who are the most suitable. For example, a successful large company executive may not be well suited to an advisory role. Conversely, some people with a non-industrial background such as the services or diplomatic corps might be able to bring considerable knowledge and contacts in an overseas country. A further potential source could be high-flyers who are presently subsidiary board directors of large groups, where their experience gives them a foretaste of working on a top board.

If a suitable shortlist is not forthcoming from the data base, Hanson Green follows the normal process of search consultants to find appropriate candidates, interview them, and then produce the final short list.

Further research into the company then follows, its industry and main competitors. Soundings might include, for example, CBI and City contacts, private sources, and public data bases such as Textline. If the individual is to help in a rescue, Hanson Green can help with a contact at Lloyds who offers director's indemnity up to £500,000.

At this stage, the client is asked to undertake a thorough review of the shortlisted candidates in light of the required contribution of the independent director, the chemistry around the board table, and time availability. It is also helpful if the candidate lives near the head office, as this makes for local knowledge and easy availability for ad hoc meetings.

It is important for a new independent director to pick up a brief quickly so that newcomers can rapidly contribute to board discussions. He should also have the courage to ask questions freely, both to learn about the company and to protect his own position.

Peter Waine emphasizes the importance of remuneration. In his view, £5,000 p.a. is inadequate for the right individual, £7,000 should be regarded as a minimum for one meeting a month, and £12,500 p.a. is a reasonable average fee. Appointments should initially be for one year, then renewable. Clients are recommended to consider the appointment of two independent directors, as it can be extremely difficult for one individual to shift the perceptions of an entrenched executive team.

An example

Hanson Green had a Japanese client, long established in the UK. Traditionally, the board was composed of a Japanese chairman, (appointed from Japan for a limited period, usually under three years) and mainly of British executive counterparts, with an average board tenure of eight years.

Hanson Green was asked to find a non-executive director to leaven a board comprised of the chairman and other directors with a limited range of commercial experience. The company chose a principal from a major British management school rather than a conventional businessman. It was a masterstroke.

The non-executive director acted as a quiet but persistent confidante for the chairman, and a catalyst for change. Doors were opened, problems highlighted, solutions offered.

Soon the board decided to appoint a second non-executive director – this time recruited from the Continent. The aim is to help create a European pool of managers and cater for the different educational and business cultures of various countries.

Sir John Trelawney, Director GKR

GKR's primary business is recruiting executives but recently there has been an increasing demand for finding independent directors.

The first contact will almost invariably be with the chairman, although the recommendations might have come from a number of other sources such as stockbrokers, or financial advisers. A senior executive will then visit the company to discuss in depth the skills and personalities around the board table and the qualities required of the proposed candidate. GKR's experience in recruiting senior executives is felt to give them an excellent insight into identifying an individual who is right for the board.

The second stage is to list possible candidates that might be either executives serving on the board of other companies or successful individuals who are already independent. Surprisingly, the process of identifying six names only takes two weeks.

Arranging interviews can be handled either directly by the company or GKR. If through the former, the candidates will be contacted directly by the chairman in order of perceived merit; if the first two names are not suitable then the search for new names continues. On the other hand, if GKR contacts the individuals directly this has the advantage that the initial explanations, and any rejections or problems of locating candidates are handled away from the client.

GKR handles some 24 recruitments a year and believes that it has an important counselling role for clients who have difficulty in being objective about the people presently around the board table. Counselling is even more important when recommendations for recruiting an independent director come from outside the company; for example, investing institutions have little experience in managing boards and need guidance on the advisability and benefits of making any new appointments.

An example

GKR was introduced to a company by one of the existing non-executive directors, who had previously seen GKR at work in recruiting a chairman to another board. The Company was in the financial services business and the Chief Executive had determined that its marketing needed further strengthening by the addition of a suitable non-executive director. This is slightly unusual as one would normally expect the Chairman to be most concerned about the composition of the board.

GKR was asked to find the new non-executive director, who should have a first-class pedigree in marketing, probably gained in a fast moving consumer goods business. He should also have been a main board director of a listed company.

As in all searches, the briefing process is crucial, and focused on personality which is often more important than for an executive position. He (or she) should be someone with whom the Chairman and Chief Executive could develop a relationship of trust and very quickly form a rapport. Part of the skill of a headhunter is assessing the type of a person who will fit into an existing boardroom.

In this instance, while marketing expertise was a key requirement, there were no formal responsibilities for the non-executive director. It is, however, very important to convey an impression about the style of the business to candidates and the way in which the Chairman and Chief Executive see the non-executive director making a contribution. The brief was discussed carefully with the client before being finalized.

During this stage, preparations for the search were in hand. The mechanics of a search for a non-executive director are somewhat different from those for an executive. As the potential candidates could come from almost anywhere, it is usual to produce a list of 10–12, giving details of cvs and a brief commentary on achievements and personalities. The list of candidates is then reviewed and divided into three categories: preferred candidates, the standbys and the rejects. Normally six to eight from the original list emerge as people who could be approached; if not, one must go back to the drawing board!

The process then resumed as for any other search, with contacts by telephone and arrangements to meet. An approach to be a non-executive director is frequently felt to be flattering. The danger, however, is that people take on the role without fully understanding the responsibilities. Part of GKR's task is therefore to ensure that they do understand the commitment they are making and that they have the time and the energy to fulfil the role. GKR produced a list of four candidates, one of whom was in fact suggested by the company itself.

The first meeting between the candidates was with the Chief Executive and Chairman independently. These meetings (not 'interviews') narrowed the shortlist of four down to two, then both met the entire Board. Not suprisingly, the candidate favoured by the Chief Executive was selected and invited to join the board.

He has now been in situ for about five months and as with any other search, GKR maintains contact with him and with the company. In the company's view, he has settled into the style of the business well and has already made a valuable contribution particularly in the area of strategic marketing.

Nigel Lewis, Director, Independent Directors Programme, 3i

Soon after 3i's founding it became apparent that on occasion it would be necessary to strengthen the board of a prospective investee company, before an investment could be made. This led naturally to the practice of using local contacts to strengthen such boards. Typically the nominee would be a director from some other company in the district, often another 3i customer, or a professional adviser. This 'local' approach is still actively used, representing over half the directors that 3i today introduces to the boards of customer companies.

In 1985, it was decided that this local approach should be augmented by holding a central register. Over the next three years, a list of 450 names was established under the direction of Gerry Richardson. All had been interviewed and their attributes coded and entered onto a simple data base. A programme of events was introduced, including receptions, seminars and dinners to provide opportunities for members to meet one another and members of 3i's staff. The result was a considerable success, with some 100 directors placed onto the boards of 3i investments in the year 1989. By any comparative standard, this was a substantial rate. However, it became clear that there were significant opportunities to improve it further.

It had been accepted from the outset that the prime aim was to find directors for companies rather than positions for directors; also that such programmes invariably have fairly low utilization rates. Nevertheless four significant points emerged:

- The 1990 appointment rate of some 50 from the central register implied that 90% of members did not find a position during the year which seemed perhaps even lower than anticipated.
- While the events were appreciated and valued as a means to meet some 3i staff and other members, there was a feeling that a larger number of appointments would be appreciated still more. This perception was plainly related to the utilization issue.
- Some high flying executives were not always ideal as independent directors in the types of company that 3i is mainly concerned with.
- The mix of skills and experience required to meet 3i's aggregate demand did not accurately match the mix found in the total register.

These factors led to a recognition that a means of profiling the register was needed within the programme.

Probably the most important single factor in determining whether an individual is appointed, is how well he or she is known to the 3i executive responsible for the case. As a result, there is advantage in minimizing the size of the register, consistent with being able to produce a good shortlist against any likely requirement. This makes it critically important to have a mix of attributes in the register that accurately matches the demand pattern.

The new system

These considerations led to certain adjustments in the way the programme operated:

1 A new computer system was introduced with some 200 codes which enabled the frequency of appointment and of shortlisting of each member to be tracked. It also enabled the profile of the total register to be assessed and compared with that of the demand.
2 A fixed registration period was in introduced. Each member is on the register for 18 months, after which he automatically lapses.
3 At the 18 months lapse point, the member's computer record and any other relevant facts are reviewed, and accordingly he is invited to re-register or not. As a result, the register contains those individuals having greater than average probability of early appointment. Those who are perfectly competent yet less suited to 3i's demand, are held on a supplementary list.
4 Loose linkages were established between members and 3i offices in their vicinity, to provide for a clearly identified internal sponsor for each member. This greatly assists in achieving appointment where a member is not known to the appointing 3i office, as does the move to a smaller, profiled register.
5 The matching process needed fundamental redesign, in the following way.

Revised matching process

Traditionally, matching systems are based on yes/no tests of whether each individual has certain required attributes, leading to a list of those meeting the requirement. In practice, this approach often produces a list of too few or too many names. In either case, further runs are needed with revised search criteria, combined with manual scrutiny of numerous files. A typical search might take a day.

The solution entailed two changes:

1 Members' attributes are classified into two levels, 'in-depth' or 'familiar'.
2 Each required attribute is given a weighting or importance, e.g. 'essential', 'highly desirable', 'desirable', 'nice to have'.

Using this approach, a search results in all the members being ranked from top to bottom, according to how closely each fits the stated search template. Manual selection is then made on the basis of the fuller information in the files.

Thus, a form of computer-aided selection results, but one that focuses on the most likely individuals. The average search now takes an hour instead of a day as a result of trading off different aspects in order to approach the ideal profile, which in practice is seldom available in full, and a more refined match emerges.

With these and other adjustments, the rate of appointment increased substantially during 1990, though it eased back somewhat as the economy slowed. In addition, the programme has become more focused, with a view to improving the relevance, fit and productivity of all concerned.

The system was further improved by clarifying the expectations of company, director and 3i at the time of appointment. 3i now initiate a letter of nomination from 3i to the director (see Appendix to this chapter), and a letter of appointment from the company to the director – all to be agreed in draft by all parties.

An example

Two years ago, 3i financed the MBO of IBIS Information Services Ltd from the owners who had founded it in 1966. It is a Direct Marketing Services company with roots in publishing, involved in the management and marketing of data bases and mailing lists to academic and business markets. Its range of activities had grown to include mail list broking, telemarketing, a 'letter shop' operation, and other activities akin to these. It is not in the consumer/junk mail sector of the market.

IBIS had a highly experienced board and management, who had worked there for many years. The company had progressed steadily, but in the harder climate of 1990, felt the need for additional finance and external advice. Following one of the regular reviews with the investment executive, 3i undertook to make additional finance available and were asked to provide a suitably experienced independent director to IBIS' board.

3i's investment executive first looked to local contacts, and also sent a request for shortlist suggestions from the Independent Directors Programme register with emphasis on sales/marketing. As David Clark, Managing Director, said, this should preferably be provided 'in a package about 10 years older than the executives', with well-rounded experience including both good times and bad.

Following more detailed discussion, the computer search finally included the following attributes and weightings:

- marketing – essential
- general management – highly desirable
- finance – highly desirable
- publishing – highly desirable
- consultancy – desirable
- organic growth – desirable
- proximity to head office – desirable
- suitable as medium company independent director – desirable
- computer systems – nice to have
- retailing – nice to have
- software – nice to have
- suitable as medium company chairman – nice to have.

The search produced a listing of the register in descending order of fit to the stated requirements. Scrutiny of the top names and files caused some to be excluded for reasons not apparent in the computer record, and led to a shortlist of five names. None of these hit every desired attribute perfectly but the names presented a range of types of variation from the perfect candidate. The details were then considered by the 3i investment executive and David Clark, leading to meetings and the eventual appointment of Harry Hemens to IBIS' board. He brought a marketing and general management background from Cadbury Schweppes and Sodastream and was an established member of 3i's register.

His first problem was to satisfy the natural concerns of the existing directors that he was on their side and not a 3i spy. This is how he worked:

1 His independence had to be demonstrated. David Clark had expressed the wish that he should not be in any sense the MD's man. Hemens demonstrated this and he also showed that he was not 3i's stooge either; nor would he 'go native' in taking the point of view of management to the exclusion of the other parties.
2 He demonstrated the ability to listen, and to do so with various different levels and groupings in a way that respected the confidentiality of all and left a feeling of trust and confidence. In this, he was helped by a well-thought-out introduction programme, which set up appropriate initial expectations of his role and relationships.
3 He focused IBIS' attention heavily on the customer and the customer's needs of IBIS. Much time was spent in the early stages on meetings with customers. This directed the company's attention to what they should offer, how IBIS could best organize to

meet customer needs, and how its performance in this area could be measured.

4 He worked to clarify and refine the management and communication processes, so that the roles of board and executives were clearly defined and distinguished.

Before long, it became clear that Harry Hemens would be able to make a major further contribution in the sales/marketing area, if he could spend more time than the 'monthly board meeting plus' that is normally required from an independent director. For a finite period, therefore, he was retained to provide additional time.

Appendix

Example letter of Nomination from 3i to Nominee
YOUR APPOINTMENT AS CHAIRMAN [/DIRECTOR] OF XYZ LTD

Dear . . . . ,

3i has the right to nominate a Director [who shall be chairman] to the Board of XYZ Ltd and is pleased to ask you to undertake this post. This appointment is supported by the other shareholders [who are in fact the directors] and will be subject to formal confirmation in general meeting. [The terms of your nomination and appointment as a non-executive director of this company are contained in an agreement/the Company's articles of which I enclose copies.]

The purpose of this letter which has been discussed with the Company, is to set out the basis of your nomination and the role that 3i envisages.

1. First and foremost, although you have been nominated by 3i your obligations and responsibilities are to the company, and like other directors you should act at all times in what you consider to be the best interests of the Company. You should exercise your independent judgement on all matters. While 3i expects you to have regard to its interests it recognizes that your primary obligations are to the Company and it will not seek to instruct or direct you nor are you under any obligation to act in accordance with 3i's wishes.

2. Your position is that of non-executive director [/Chairman]. Since, legally there is no distinction between the duties of directors, you will owe all the normal duties which a director owes to a company. It is expected that you will attend all board meetings and take whatever steps may be necessary to ensure that you have sufficient knowledge and familiarity with the Company's affairs to discharge the duties which your position entails.

[The time involvement on your part will to a large extent be determined by events within the Company. As a minimum however, it is expected that the board will meet officially once a quarter and unofficially with senior management once a month.]

[3. The primary functions envisaged are to:–

(a) Catalyse the strategic thinking in the Company and widen the horizons within which the board determines strategy; to ensure that appropriate objectives are adopted; to guard against any tendency towards managerial introversion;

(b) Procure that resources, especially finance and staff, are available to the Company consistent with its objectives;

(c) Ensure that the Company's financial reporting disciplines are in place and working adequately;

(d) Monitor management performance and the extent to which management is achieving the objectives planned when strategy was determined;

(e) Ensure that the board has adequate systems to safeguard the interests of the company where these may conflict with the personal interests of individual directors e.g. to exercise a duty to the Company in such areas as board remuneration.]

[4. You will [will not] be required to hold a share qualification (of . . .).]

5. While your nomination as 3i's nominee may be withdrawn at any time without compensation from 3i, the intended duration is 2[3] years from today's date. At that point, 3i will review the position with yourself and the Company and will inform you whether it wishes you to accept renomination for a further period.

6. For as long as you remain 3i's nominee you will not be subject to retirement by rotation. Your remuneration is to be paid direct by the Company.

The list is not exhaustive and I would be happy to discuss with you any further areas you may like to raise.

This letter by its nature has to be somewhat formal in tone. May I nevertheless take the opportunity to welcome you to this role, and to wish you every success in the appointment. If I can be of any help at any point, do please feel free to contact me.

With best wishes
Yours sincerely

5

The appointment process

Joining a board can turn out either to be a pleasure or a bed of nails. A board candidate would be wise to undertake a detailed reconnaissance before ever submitting himself for interview. This chapter is designed to provide an agenda and a draft set of rules.

How is one appointed?

Most large company independent directors are senior directors already serving or who have retired from top executive positions. These people have invariably worked their way up one or more large organizations and are known by reputation to chairmen seeking new directors. This is in no way an 'old boys' network. The top individuals have proven merit and are contacted either directly or through mutual friends. Unless someone has a particular legal, financial or technical skill, it is unlikely that he will be invited onto the board of a large company without having gained direct experience of a major organization.

The choice is much wider in the second tier of small to medium companies. Potential candidates may be chosen through direct contact or through one of the following intermediaries:

- Merchant banks usually have a list of people available as independent directors whom they have known in client companies. Historically, bankers have themselves been candidates for appointment but under the latest Institutional Shareholder Committee circular, financial advisers are not deemed to be truly independent.
- Stockbrokers have also been a traditional source but are in a similar category to merchant banks.
- Clearing banks have intensive care units who keep a list of people who can help with companies in trouble. The most suitable background for this type of work is a past history of trouble shooting.
- Auditors or legal advisers used to be a source of independent directors but these suffer from a similar limitation to the merchant banks or stockbrokers.
- Venture capitalists are drawing on a similar vein as larger companies but their experience has tended to be in the smaller company sector.

There are also the professional agencies which are used if a company chairman wants a particular skill, industry knowledge or contacts. The agencies either work from a register (where each person has been interviewed and references taken) or from personal contact.

Both registry and search techniques can produce a short list quite quickly – the problem is to become a candidate. Most agencies exist through reputation and the list of candidates is continually being pruned. From a client standpoint, an agency with a comprehensive register such as Pro Ned can produce a shortlist in about three weeks.

How should one respond to an interview request?

With pleasure but with some caution. Reputations are quickly broken if an individual is seen to go on the board of a company which fails within a short time, but there are exceptions. These are professional company doctors appointed to rescue companies who will only go into a situation supported by either the major institutions or banks. Sometimes even they find the situation still more hopeless than anyone realized and have to recommend receivership as the best solution.

Experienced individuals will spend much time researching a business before the first meeting. It does not enhance anyone's reputation to reject a company after meeting the chairman or chief executive because details were missed on the initial analysis. If the contact is through an agency much of the preliminary work should have been done – their reputation is also at stake and most are paid on results.

Whatever the introduction, time spent in reconnaissance is seldom wasted. Being a director of a company is a serious commitment and the candidate is at the start of a steep learning curve.

Sources of reference information

- Glean whatever information is available from the mutual contact. If a stockbroker or merchant bank, the file will contain several years' report and accounts, stockbrokers' circulars and perhaps press releases.
- The report and accounts for listed companies are available from the Registrars or from Companies House for non-listed companies. Where a company has been losing money, details can often be found from subsidiary micro-fiches.
- The accounting data for several years' annual accounts should be set out in columns and the critical ratios calculated for each year. If there are major question marks, check the credit rating with Syspas or another agency (see References).
- Trade enquiries can be made either directly or indirectly. More details can be gained from the sales literature, trade directories, and journals.
- City or local contacts are useful cross-references even if these were not the source of the original enquiry. Merchant banks, stockbrokers, auditors or legal advisers, can often provide important background information.
- Evaluate the business and list the strengths and weaknesses. It is good practice to exchange the conclusions with a colleague.

- Memorize the salient points and prepare a list of questions for the chairman or whoever is the first contact.

The first meeting

By now the candidate will have come to a number of preliminary conclusions which will either be confirmed or varied at the interview. It would be wise to consider this from both aspects.

From the standpoint of the candidate

- Most independent directors do not get especially well paid so the business has to be interesting. Is it worth the time?
- Is the company sound? During the interview it would be wise to check any possible misgivings about the company's status and prospects.
- How does the chairman run the company, how is he likely to utilize the skills of the independent director(s)?
- Would the appointment require service on the audit or remuneration committees? Other duties may be specified.
- Check the induction procedures. This should include visiting subsidiary companies, meeting senior managers and learning about the business. Such an approach should be welcomed by the company; there should be suspicion if it is resisted.
- Can time be spared to do the appointment justice?
- There should be a good understanding of the board chemistry after meeting both the executive and independent directors. Could the newcomer's name be safely added to a document such as a rights issue.

The view from the company

The interviewer may have a different set of priorities depending upon the standpoint of the chairman and other directors. It is also likely that there will be other candidates and a short list will entail further meetings. These are some of the likely headings on the agenda:

- Will personalities fit around the board table? A good chairman will welcome informed contributions, but someone who feels moved to comment on each item may not be welcomed.
- In some cases, the chairman will be looking for a confidante as well as a colleague. Will the candidate be seen as a possible rival?
- How much does the candidate know about the business or will everything have to be learned from scratch? Will he bring useful contacts?
- What system of assessment will be used? Will the interviewer go through the candidate's track record in detail or will his judgement be tested in several situations?
- Are there special skills needed? For example, if the company is going through a rough patch, will the candidate have to operate as a company doctor?

The candidate should feel encouraged if the interview procedure has been thought out and is thorough. This would indicate that the chairman is taking the appointment seriously and is genuinely anxious to find the right person.

The appointment

The candidate has emerged successfully from the interview procedure; he is also happy to be associated with the business, the company and the board. This is the form of appointment procedure that may be expected either from a listed company or as a nominee from a venture capitalist.

Appointment by a board

Pro Ned have suggested a list of items that should be included in a modern letter of appointment:

- The date and locations of board meetings.
- Appointment to any of the board sub-committees, how often they meet, the names of the officers.

- Duration of appointment and the ratification procedures by shareholders.
- Fees, usually paid monthly and expenses. Some companies now offer to pay legal expenses of independent directors incurred in the course of their duties. This could be a matter of some delicacy because legal advice could imply boardroom conflict.
- The contact for obtaining joining material, arranging meetings with senior executives and visiting sites etc.

Appointment through an intermediary

There may be three parties to the appointment: the venture capitalist (or other provider of capital); the company executives (who may be the majority shareholders); and the independent director.

First

The fund providers will have evaluated the strengths and weaknesses of the executive directors and shareholders at the time of considering the deal. The situations will vary depending upon the situation. For example, in a buy-out, the directors will understand the industry but may not have had dealings with independent shareholders.

Second

Depending upon the circumstances, the venture capitalist will agree with the executive directors the nature of the proposed appointment and a short list of suggested individuals. Ideally, the candidates will be personally known to the investment executive but in other cases, names may have come from a list or register and the investment executive will have to check with a third party.

Third

After interviews, the executive directors should have agreed on the chosen nominee.

Fourth

Assuming the candidate also still wishes to proceed, the investment executive should write setting out the duties and responsibilities of the new director and a summary of what is expected from the individual.

Fifth

The company should then write a letter to the candidate setting out details of the appointment which will contain a similar pattern to that of Pro Ned but without some of the details.

Joining the board

The new director is now at the start of a steep learning curve and there should be a major opportunity to meet people, learn about the business, visit sites, learn procedures etc. Attention should also be paid to important issues such as who is the cheque-signing authority, how cash is handled etc.

This initial period is important. During this time the new director should ask all the simple questions that will not be tolerated six months later. After the initial period the newcomer will be deemed by his board colleagues, and those outside the company, to have made it his business to know and understand the company – warts and all!

Some farsighted companies set their new directors a joining task of making an investigation or reporting on internal matters as part of their introduction. This works two ways. The individual is given a specific brief arising from visits and meetings; the company may learn something both about itself and the new director.

The first board meeting

The new director should prepare for his first board meeting with considerable care and thought. If meeting procedures are familiar, the routine of dealing with the previous minutes, matters arising etc. will be well understood. What will be unfamiliar is the way the board conducts its affairs and the interaction of the personalities.

- Arrive in good time.
- Go through the board papers in detail. Much will be unfamiliar and any questions should be discussed before the meeting with the appropriate director so as not to waste the board's time.
- There may be items on the agenda which may be of immediate concern to the new director. The matter should be discussed with the chairman beforehand.
- When in doubt a new director should say little unless the matter is of particular interest.

A new director should be conscious of first impressions which work both ways:

- Notice the seating arrangement around the board table, the lighting, the chairman's position, and shape of the table.
- Observe the interaction of individuals. The conflicting objectives of the production and sales people are well known – but there may be other groups. Do they see eye to eye on all issues?
- What contribution is required from the outside directors? Does the chairman deliberately bring them into the debate or do they play a purely peripheral role?
- Consider how issues are dealt with and concluded at a meeting. Badly run boards have many 'matters arising' going back in time because the chairman has been unable to deal with the items effectively.
- Do not feel everyone has to speak or question every issue just to show they are alert. Colleagues will welcome silence unless there is something important to say.
- It is possible that there is an inner circle of directors who know that something is amiss in the company and wish it kept quiet. In particular, notice if matters that should be discussed like uncorrected losses, or contract failures are set aside for less important items such as small items of capital expenditure.
- At the end of the meeting, the chairman might ask a new director for his private response to individual contributions. Be ready!
- The chairman may not be the only one who wants your opinions

or support. Be on the look out for other factions.

These considerations can be summarized in thirteen rules:

Rule 1. Anyone wanting/wishing to serve on a board should first undertake an apprenticeship. Few companies now want names just to ornament the writing paper. They want individuals able and competent to make a specific contribution to the future direction and the efficient running of the business.

Rule 2. The apprenticeship should have been served either in industry or commerce or in one of the professions. Board membership requires an individual to contribute to a wide range of topics, not just to a narrow specialization.

Rule 3. The apprenticeship should have taken the individual to board level as an executive. He should have moved out of a narrow specialization and have spent some time in general management.

Rule 4. Time spent in reconnaissance is seldom wasted. Learn as much as possible about the company and the directors before meeting members of the board.

Rule 5. Consider the most likely contribution of a new outside director and list the questions to be asked at an interview.

Rule 6. At the first meeting, check as many of the points arising from your initial analysis as possible. Build up a profile of potential board colleagues. Remember, interviews work two ways – both parties have to be satisfied.

Rule 7. When appointed, use the first six months to learn as much about the business as possible. The size of the business will define how much can be assimilated but use the time to absorb the answers to basic questions, a similar opportunity may not occur again.

Work around the board table varies from company to company and in different stages of development. For example, a newly formed business or a buy-out will concentrate on totally different issues from a settled PLC. Consider these further factors:

Rule 8. Note how the board operates. Each board will be run in a different way depending upon personalities, tradition, relationships, possible cabals etc.

Rule 9. Do not just rely on the board papers to assess progress, look behind the reports and remember that it is not possible to 'learn where a ship is going by gazing at the wake'. Study the critical factors that drive the added value of the business and the leading indicators that spell future success or failure. Remember that by the time a problem hits the operating statement it may be too late to take remedial action.

Rule 10. Play a full part in the board sub-committees or other nominated work as required by the chairman. Also remember that the first duty of the board is to generate a strategy to which each member can be committed.

Rule 11. Keep in touch with the 'sharp end' by visiting subsidiaries, offices, factories or going out with salesmen, having first made the appointments through the executives. Also try to visit exhibitions where the company has a stand.

Rule 12. Although an independent director should be working and cooperating with the executives he also has a duty to assure himself that the business is being run efficiently and honestly. It may sometimes be difficult to make the needed enquiries against executive blandishments or withheld information.

Rule 13. Independent directors may be required to take a higher profile than normal if either shareholders or creditors become dissatisfied with executive performance and demand changes. Internal dissent is to be avoided wherever possible but independent directors have a clear duty to monitor executive performance on behalf of shareholders, creditors and staff.

6

Essential checks when joining a board (due diligence)

It is said that Mikhail Gorbachev told this story:

'Bush has 100 secret service guards. One is a potential assassin – but which one? Gorbachev has 100 economists. Only one knows what he is talking about – but which one?'

To which some independent directors might add:

'Most executive directors are competent and trustworthy. Some are incompetent and may not be telling the truth – but which ones?'

No shareholder can sensibly expect an independent director to know as much about a company as the executives; the most they can reasonably expect is for an individual not to be afraid to ask the right question and become informed. He should not assume something is correct, he should check it out.

Learning about a new business means absorbing much new information, some of it vital, some less important. There follows a suggested list of headings that should be checked out at the stage of joining a new board. The general issue of required regular board information is outside the scope of this book, but an illustrative outline extract is attached as an appendix to this chapter.

Most of what is written here can only be learnt through experience and many independent directors will have been through their own traumas and have their own questions.

The list is designed for a small to medium sized business where the board has regular details of subsidiaries. Independent directors of large companies will need some adjustments.

The headings are designed to be directed to a number of different individuals in the company; for example, questions relating to the Memorandum and Articles should obviously be directed towards the company secretary. There are 15 headings which are organized in no particular order.

1 The Memorandum and Articles of Association are the legal framework in which a company is regulated within the company law. These are some of the matters for enquiry with the Secretary:

- Have the documents been brought up to date if required by recent regulations?
- Are there any restrictions on the company's activities?
- How many directors are allowed and are there any restrictions placed upon the board?
- What is the procedure for appointing and removing directors?

2 How much is known about the chairman, executives and independent directors? What do they receive from the company?

- Are curriculum vitae available, what is their track record, what are their qualifications and how were they appointed?
- What other directorships are held, have these been declared to the board, do any of the board have business dealings with the company?
- What are their service contracts (if any), salary, bonus payments, share options, commissions, car and fixed expense allowances?
- How are the emoluments and benefits agreed, is there a Chairman's or Emoluments Committee and who sits on it?

3 What authority does each member of the board possess?

- Who is responsible for authorizing and signing directors' expenses?
- Whose signature is required for drawing cheques on the company? What are the limitations without board approval? How are the approvals recorded?
- Have depositories for the company's cash been agreed, who has the authority to move cash and up to what value without board approval?
- How are major items of capital or revenue expenditure authorized?

4 What is known about the company's banking relationships?

- How many banks are involved, is there a lead bank and who is responsible for the treasury function?
- What is allowed by the bank mandates? What are the borrowing limits and covenant limitations? Are these reported with the board papers?
- What collateral and security do the banks have over the company's assets? Are there cross guarantees between subsidiaries that would limit asset or company disposals without creditor permission?
- Is performance against covenants and limits reported regularly to the board? What is reported to the banks?

5 Shareholders may be large institutions that take great interest in the company, an individual holding a large block who is a potential seller, executives, or a series of disinterested groups or individuals.

- Who are the major shareholders, have they a spokesman and have they signalled any specific objectives?
- Are they represented by any investment committee?
- Does the board have any communication with them apart from the interim and preliminary statements and AGM? Does the chairman make himself available for meetings with analysts or discussions of strategy?
- Has the board discussed and implemented the various discussion documents from the Institutional Shareholders Committee and other Shareholders Committees?
- Are there large blocks of shares on sale which might alter future ownership?

- Are there special conditions from certain shareholders such as venture capitalists?
- If venture capitalists are syndicated, have all shareholders the same objectives, if not what are the attitudes of each of the players? What is the contact point with each investor?
- Is there a potential bidder owning a large holding?

6 The standards of accounting or auditing have been questioned after some large companies failed in the early 1990s.

- Who are the auditors and what is their track record?
- Who are the financial advisers and stockbrokers?
- If the company has overseas subsidiaries, are these audited by local firms whose standards are lower than might be acceptable in the UK or USA?
- Does the company have an audit committee, who sits on it and how rigorous is its examination of the accounts? If it is a financial services company, who sits on the compliance committee and do they have confidential access to the relevant officers?
- How is the inventory valued, who values it, how much profit is included and have any obsolescent items been written down or off? If a contracting business, what attempts have been made to value the work-in-progress against acceptance by clients?
- If a contracting company, is there a performance bond, who holds it and how can it be redeemed?
- How closely do the major items in the receivables tally with the debtors? What is the stated and actual collection period and what is the debtor ageing profile? How many of the late payers are held up through non-acceptance of credit notes?
- Is cash deposited in secure banks, does the company take steps to insure currency risks?
- Are the creditors correctly stated, are there any liabilities such as contract penalties, possible litigation or risks that have not been recorded?
- Are there off-balance sheet liabilities that could pose a threat to the company, is board approval needed for major items and who is responsible for monitoring them?
- What are the age and valuations of the major fixed asset items? Are the property or machinery assets fully utilized, what are the items that may be spare and are there any disposal limitations?

- If the company possesses luxury items such as aeroplanes or yachts, where do these appear in the balance sheet?

7 Complete, accurate and timely board papers are an essential part of conducting a board meeting effectively and getting the most value from the directors in the time available.

- Is the operating statement submitted against budget with comparisons against the previous year?
- Is a pro-forma balance sheet presented together with a cash-flow statement? Are ratios presented concerning debtor ageing and inventory turnround and are explanations given for the problems and rectification action described?
- Are performances shown against bank limits and covenants?
- Are the statements provided by the chief executive and other executive directors to the point, pre-answering most questions?
- Do the agenda regularly bring up the same item(s) unresolved from previous meetings; why have these not been dealt with?
- Is there a regular item on the agenda concerning developing board strategy and progress along a charted path?

8 Part of an independent director's duty is to understand what drives the company's added value.

- What are the company's major product lines? At what stage are their life cycles and what development work is undertaken to continue their profitable life or develop new lines? This should be considered in conjunction with Chapter 10.
- Are the major product lines of a company, division, activity or group regularly calculated? What are the gross and net margins after overheads have been allocated? What is the return on assets once these have been divided?
- If a service or contracting company, how is the added value calculated and what action is taken to retain competitiveness? Who is responsible for maintaining added value and how are resources allocated?
- What use is made of licensing and other joint venture techniques?
- Are any major changes in policy submitted to the board for approval? To be successful, a company needs to win and retain customers. How much is known about the major accounts

around the board table and how secure is the continuing cash flow?

9 It is a matter of principle that when problems 'hit the operating statement' it is often too late to take action.

- What leading indicators are used to give early warning of opportunities or problems? Whose job is it to monitor and report changes?
- If leading indicators are not reported specifically, they may be understood by certain executives. For example, there may be a historical causal relationship between rising (or falling) interest rates and offtake from builders merchants.
- If the leading indicators are not officially recorded, whose job is it to note any changes and take action?

10 Marketing and sales policy.

- Which are the major accounts in each company, division etc., what is the offtake and who has account responsibility?
- Who establishes the commercial policy towards customers, how does this affect defining direct or distributor sales, small orders, discounts, collection etc? Who has responsibility for changing the policy and how is this monitored?
- Are the major accounts under the control of a senior individual; what is the back-up in the event of the person leaving for any reason?
- Is any consideration given to using other marketing techniques such as licensing or franchising?

11 What part does the weather play in corporate decisions?

- What important decisions are weather related? For example, are fashions or designs changed on the assumption that the weather will change?
- Who takes these decisions and what amounts of cash do these involve?
- Does the company try to improve the quality of the weather-related input?

12 Except for the smallest, most companies have subsidiaries run

by non-board members who have direct control over major aspects of profitability and cash flow. Visiting these companies should be part of an independent director's induction procedure.

- Meet the management and ask relevant questions about the history of the business, present main activities, current state of play, the major competitors and the policy for maintaining a competitive edge.
- How does the group control subsidiary managers, is the group executive director the subsidiary chairman and what reporting is required? How good is group support, what is included in the group service charge and is it deemed to be fair?
- Are the factories, warehouses and offices in good condition? Is there a good feeling, are people busy, is the general age and condition of the plant good and well utilized? Is there a large amount of inventory around? Is the general morale of the workpeople good, what unions are involved etc?
- Look through the cost and financial accounts and gauge their value as a management system.

13 Whatever the size of company someone has to be responsible for the health and safety regulations and the requirements under the employment acts.

- Are the regulations handled within the company or through an agency? Who is the responsible executive? Have there been any problems with the inspectors?
- What unions are involved, who is responsible for negotiating with officials, dispute procedures etc?
- What are the personnel policies for recruitment, training, management succession, dismissals etc?
- How are salary levels and bonuses fixed, is there a company-wide policy or are matters arranged locally?

14 When a company goes off the rails and starts to make losses, one of the first things a newcomer does is to prise open the budget assumptions, then put these back together in a realistic manner. Shareholders can reasonably ask why someone new did not challenge misleading data.

- Do the executives have any idea that a business cycle exists and at what point the company is trading (see Chapter 10). Check the condition of the leading indicators that signal expansion or potential caution.

- What are the assumptions behind the sales figures? Why should these vary from a previous year taking into account demand, competition, spending, tariff protection, consumer preferences, technical factors etc?
- Have costs expanded in line with the assumed sales expansion? Are these variable costs that rise and fall with volume or fixed and potentially expensive to reduce?
- What are the sensitivities behind the assumptions, what difference will a volume rise or fall of 5, 10 or 15% make to the expected result? At what point will the board make a decision to retrench if the expected budget figures are not met? At what point will this be communicated to bankers and shareholders?
- Will any retrenchment mean recasting the budget or just leaving the previous assumptions in place hoping that growth would be resumed?
- Have the over-optimistic sales assumptions weakened the balance sheet through overborrowing – just at the time when interest rates were rising? Is it possible to redress the situation by reducing inventory or other assets to pay off debt?

15 Unwise and untimely acquisitions and diversifications have been the downfall for many companies, it seems that each generation of executives has to learn the danger of overexpansion towards the end of the business cycle when optimism abounds.

This presents a major problem for the outside director who may sense something is wrong but is reluctant to challenge a confident and (supposedly) competent chief executive. In these circumstances, the best that an independent director can do is to test the reasoning behind the proposal and complain if not satisfied with the replies. If the matter is sufficiently critical, it may be a question of minuting a complaint or, in the last resort, resigning.

- How much is known about the proposal? Is this part of an agreed strategy or an opportunistic effort to increase earnings per share?
- What contribution will the initiative make to sales, profits and the balance sheet? Which particular part of the business will

benefit synergistically, how will these advantages be managed, by whom and over what time scale?

- Is the initiative to be made in a part of the world where the company has any experience? For example, what are the working conditions for staff, how will payments be arranged, what are the arrangements for sending out equipment and materials, will there be local support and liaison?

- If there is to be overseas acquisition, can we rely on the audited accounts; were the books kept for the benefit of the share-holders, the tax man or the directors; will the best people leave once they have received their money? How difficult is it, and how expensive might it be to reduce costs, will it really receive a benefit from the present operations or will the newcomer work alone? How much management time might it need in sorting it out?

- How is the deal to be financed? If on borrowings, how are these to be repaid; if on equity, how will this dilute shareholders funds? How solvent is the company and can we avoid cross-guarantees if the acquisition proves a disaster? Is there a commitment to put in more funds and at what point could one walk away from the arrangement without paying a large compensation?

Appendix:
Illustrative outline extract of required board information

ENIGMA HOLDINGS CO. LTD
MANAGING DIRECTOR'S REPORT

1 The Finance Director's and Operations Director's reports for 48 weeks' trading are attached. As noted in the previous report, the effect of bad weather, the recession and closures for security reasons, combined to reduce sales markedly.

2 The business has conducted an intensive review into the organization structure and staffing levels of the Brand, Support Services and Administration functions, to seek to reduce overheads in line with sales trends.

As a result, a revised structure will be put into operation for the 1991/92 financial year, with 30 fewer posts in the establishment. The full year saving, apart from the one-off costs of implementation, will be in the order of £450k. Other areas of costs are also being re-examined to see if further economies can be effected.

3 Negotiations with the Landlords over lease renewals have made no significant progress to date, but are continuing. We shall be investigating methods of compensation for loss of profit due to the security closures mentioned above with the Property companies. We have also advised them that all non-essential capital expenditure will be suspended for a 3-month period.

FINANCE DIRECTORS' REPORT

1 *Group Profit and Loss Account*
Sales in the period were £5,380,000, £892,000 (14.2%) below budget and £624,000 (10.4%) below the corresponding period last year.

The adverse effects of the abnormal trading situation brought about by the extreme weather conditions in weeks 45 and 46 compounded the effects of the ongoing deteriorating volume situation.

The period gross margin fell slightly from 67% in period 11, to 66.9% in period 12. The cumulative margin at 67.1% is now 0.1% below budget.

Efficiency savings were achieved in most categories of cost, except services, where the impact of winter utility charges contributed to the adverse variance of £19,000. Services costs are £48,000 less than budget for the year to date.

In summary, the business made a pre-tax loss of £40,000, £217,000 worse than budget with cost savings largely off-setting the shortfall in budgeting revenue of £892,000.

In view of the above and the ongoing impact of closures in period 13, the half-year forecast is now thought to be at risk, possibly by some £200,000.

2 *Balance Sheet and Funds Flow*

The unbudgeted debtor increase is offset by a matching creditor increase relating to construction costs in Big Eats. Interest accruals have reduced from the period 12 level following payments of both mezzanine and senior loan interest. The interest Fixed Rate Agreement has benefited the business by £11,000 for the period March to May 1991.

The funds flow period variances on debtors and creditors relate to Big Eats as stated above. The prepayment variance of £1m is offset in accruals and relates to rental payments still being in arrears. The remaining accruals variance is accounted for by a reduction in capital expenditure liabilities and clearance of disputed invoices.

The rolling cash flow forecast has been amended to reflect the new VAT rate of 17.5% with effect from 1 April 1991.

OPERATIONS DIRECTOR'S REPORT

Retail
Sales in the period fell short of budget by £46k. The improvement in gross percentage was principally achieved through changes in the sales mix. Salaries and wages were in line with budget. This Brand is now managed by the Grazers Brand Manager.

Big Eats
With the majority of units based in London, this Brand was badly affected by the security situation and there have been continual closures at the weekends and early mornings as a result of hoax callers. Gross profit percentage again improved as product changes and control measures began to take full effect. Tight rostering produced a significant saving on salaries and wages costs.

Happy Hour
With most units in this Brand not opening until mid-morning, the security alarms did not have as much effect on sales. Gross profit percentage fell despite an excellent control result and this will be investigated by the Brand Manager.

Jemima's Pantry

This entire Brand is based in London. Of the £892k national sales shortfall, 45% was attributable to this Brand. The Oven Fresh Brand again held up well in sales terms given the situation. Average spend, gross profit percentage, salaries and wages savings, all improved in the period.

Grazers

Sales in this Brand were up on the previous period by £131k. The revenue shortfall against budget was in line with period 10. Average spend increased by 3p in the period. Further action is required on salaries and wages control.

7

Investigating a company's accounts

John Jarvis and James Chalmers
Coopers & Lybrand Deloitte

Introduction

Independent directors are required to show the same duty of care and fiduciary duty to a company as the executive directors of that company. They will be subject to the same liabilities as any other director in relation to compensating their company for loss arising out of their duties, and also in relation to disqualification. In law, they have the same responsibilities as the executive directors in connection with the accounts of the company.

Independent directors should therefore ensure that they have the same access to information within the company as other directors.

As independent directors they can make certain other contributions to the board. The Institute of Directors, in its booklet *Guidelines for Directors* (1990) describes the contributions their independence can make. These can be summarized as:

- To bring wider general or special experience into board discussions.

- To monitor management performance against its stated strategy.
- To ensure adequate systems to safeguard the interests of the company where these may conflict with the personal interest of directors, for instance in areas of board appointments and remuneration; and to ensure that the financial information available to the board is adequate.

If an independent director considers that insufficient financial information is available to the board, it is his duty to bring it to the attention of the board.

This chapter sets out the independent director's responsibilities in connection with the accounts of a company, provides guidance on how he should carry out those responsibilities and outlines what action he might take in the event that he suspects that there may be financial problems within the company.

Accounting and financial responsibilities

Responsibilities

The directors of a company are responsible for the preparation of accounts for each financial year, consisting of a balance sheet and a profit and loss account and related notes, which comply with the requirements of the Companies Act 1985. In addition to the requirement to prepare annual accounts the directors also have a duty under the Act:

- To ensure that accounting records sufficient to show and explain the company's transactions are maintained.
- In addition to preparing them, to approve the annual accounts which comply with the requirements of the 1985 Act.
- To ensure that the company sends copies of the annual accounts, the directors' report and the auditors' report to every shareholder and other person entitled to receive them.
- To lay annual accounts, the directors' report and the auditors' report before shareholders in general meeting (unless the company, as a private company, has validly elected to dispense with the laying of accounts).
- To deliver the accounts, the directors' report and the auditors'

report to the registrar of companies within the period permitted by the Companies Act 1985.

The statutory requirements set out above are generally considered to be the minimum requirements with regard to a company's accounting system. Established or larger businesses are likely to have sophisticated computerized systems which will provide statistical and management information as well as the financial information that is required for the preparation of the annual accounts. However, whatever the nature of a company's systems, they must be sufficient to provide the directors with such information as is necessary for them to discharge their duties as directors. Internal controls should, therefore, be established by the management in order to carry on the business of a company in an orderly and efficient manner, to ensure adherence to management policies and safeguard the assets, as well as to secure as far as possible the completeness and accuracy of the records. The exact procedures adopted by the company will depend on its size, scope and nature.

Proper accounting records

Every company is required to keep proper accounting records. The accounting records must be sufficient to show and explain the company's transactions and, consequently, to disclose with reasonable accuracy the company's financial position at any time; and enable the directors to ensure that any balance sheet and profit and loss account prepared from the accounting records comply with the requirements of the Companies Act 1985. In particular the accounting records should contain:

- Daily records of cash and receipts and payments together with explanations of what they were for.
- A record of the assets and liabilities of the company.
- Where the company deals in goods, a full list of the stock held at the year-end and the underlying stocktake records from which the list was prepared.
- Details of all goods sold and purchased by the company in sufficient detail to enable the goods and the buyers and sellers to be identified. (This requirement, however, does not apply to companies carrying on retail trades.)

The Institute of Chartered Accountants in England and Wales has provided the following guidance in relation to best practice.

'In addition to the statutory requirement to keep proper accounting records, the directors have an overriding responsibility to ensure that they have adequate information to enable them to discharge their duty to manage the company's business.

'The duty to manage the company's business will involve ensuring that adequate control is kept over its records and transactions, for example:

a Cash.
b Debtors and creditors.
c Stock and work in progress.
d Capital expenditure.
e Major contracts.

'The nature and extent of the accounting and management information needed to exercise this control will depend upon the nature and extent of the company's business.

'To restrict the possibility of actions for wrongful trading, directors will constantly need to be aware of the company's financial position and progress, and the accounting records should be sufficient to enable them to be provided with the information required for drawing conclusions on these matters. The directors should also be satisfied that proper systems to provide them with regular and prompt information are in place.

'Directors must also be aware of a company's prospects. It may therefore be prudent to prepare a plan against which the subsequent performance of the business can be measured. Periodic management accounts assist in enabling the actual operating results and cash position to be compared with the plan. Once again, the need for, extent and frequency of the preparation of such accounts and the level of management to which they are presented will depend upon the size, scope and nature of the business. However, the directors' report on the financial statements must contain an indication of the likely future developments in the business of the company and its subsidiaries (Companies Act 1985, Schedule 7), and a plan is likely to be helpful in this context.'

In practice, a company's normal accounting records would include:

- Cash book.
- Sales day book.
- Sales return book.
- Purchase day book.
- Creditors' ledger.
- Debtors' ledger.
- Transfer journal.
- General ledger.

These records may be retained in book form, or on computers or in any other suitable readable form. Other books of account may be used to assist directors in the preparation of management accounts.

Customs & Excise and the Inland Revenue also place certain requirements on companies to maintain accounting records. These are not detailed in this chapter.

Financial information available to the director

Under normal circumstances an independent director will only receive the financial information presented at board meetings. This information may vary considerably in its nature, content and frequency from one company to another. Typically during the course of a year the following financial information will be put before the board:

- Management accounts (at each meeting).
- Budget or plan for future (whenever prepared and ready for discussion – typically annually).
- Statutory accounts for approval.
- One-off financial reports.

As a director of the company an independent director has access to further information should he require it. However, in a well-managed company, this will not normally be necessary.

Management accounts

Management accounts are not governed by any particular legislation or accounting standards. However, they should be sufficient to provide directors with adequate information to enable them to discharge their duty to manage the business. Management accounts, as their name would suggest, are one of the tools used by management to monitor the performance of a business.

Typically management accounts comprise:

- Profit and loss account (trading and contribution statement).
- Balance sheet.
- Cash flow statement.
- Major contract summary.
- Capital expenditure summary.

This information would be given for each major division of a company/group and in consolidated form to show the performance of the company/group as a whole. The exact format of the management accounts would depend on the size and nature of the company concerned.

Management accounts would normally show the results for the period since the previous set of management accounts were prepared (typically four weeks or a calendar month), together with the cumulative results to date for the current financial year. Both the monthly and year-to-date figures would be compared with the budgets for the respective periods and actuals for the previous financial year.

Budgets

Once or twice a year a well-managed company will undergo a full-scale budgeting exercise. This would normally be prepared on a 'bottom-up' basis, i.e. built up from budget submissions from each profit centre, aggregated, discussed and approved at divisional level and then consolidated for presentation to the board for final discussion and approval. The budget would normally be presented in a similar format to the monthly management accounts. There are two reasons for using a consistent format; first so that the directors will be familiar with its overall layout of the budget and second so that the budget can be easily incorporated into future periods' management accounts. There are many styles of budgeting, 'last year's figures' plus 15% is of little use to anyone. One method is zero-based budgeting in which each activity is justified, and then costed, from scratch each year. This approach has many strong supporters.

Statutory accounts

Although independent directors will not normally be involved in the preparation of the statutory accounts they are, together with the other directors, collectively responsible for their preparation approval and filing with the Registrar. The statutory accounts comprise:

- A profit and loss account for the year.
- A balance sheet as at the last date of the company's financial year.
- A cash flow statement for the year.
- Consolidated accounts, where a company has subsidiaries at the year end.
- Notes to the accounts, which provide additional disclosure required by the Companies Act 1985 and applicable Accounting Standards in the United Kingdom.

The directors' collective responsibility for the accounts is reinforced by the legal requirement that the accounts must be approved by the board and then one of the directors of the company must sign its balance sheet on behalf of the board.

One-off financial reports

The fourth category of financial information that might be presented would be 'one-off' reports dealing with matters such as the feasibility/viability of potential acquisitions or disposals and specially commissioned investigations into particular problems identified at previous board meetings, for example, stock losses at a particular warehouse.

This type of financial information is not covered in this chapter.

Limitations of accounting information

Before considering the financial reports in detail we must first consider the limitations inherent in accounting information.

Historical vs budget

Historical information will, by its nature, be more accurate than budget information. However, in practice it is the budget information that will be far more useful to directors. At a board meeting consideration will certainly be given to the performance of the company in previous periods, particularly the most recent period, but the directors' primary concern will be with decisions which affect the performance of the company in future. It is therefore important that directors recognize that when they are looking at budgeted information they are looking at information which is based on a series of assumptions. Some of these assumptions may be very sensible with little risk of being wrong while others could be rather more speculative and therefore risky.

Speed vs accuracy

The more up to date the information given to directors the more useful it is to them in making their decisions. Certain companies are able to provide extremely accurate management information on a very timely basis, this is normally possible where a company has very sophisticated computer and accounting systems. A typical example of such a company might be a highly computerized retail organization which logs the sales at each of its shops during the day and then transmits that information to a central computer accounting function at the close of business thereby enabling a calculation of the day's profits to be made overnight. However, even with a system such as this, certain estimates must be made in order to achieve such timely results. In this particular example a typical estimate that would have to be made would be gross profit percentage. The company would determine its sales on an actuals basis as already described and then by attributing an estimate of gross profit percentage to these sales determine the cost of sales and gross profit. This type of estimate recognizes that it is impractical to perform a full stocktake at each location every day and that the benefit of timely estimated information outweighs the drawbacks that are associated with the estimates themselves or with the delays that would be inevitable if only actual data were used. The limitation of this particular approach is that management accounts will not necessarily reflect actual performance if the estimates made turn out to be erroneous.

In any company, estimates will be made in providing management accounting information. The degree and scale of these estimates will depend both on the quality of the company's accounting systems and on the speed with which the results are required. Directors should, therefore, be aware of the trade-off between timely information and the accuracy of that information and ensure that they are aware of and if necessary question the basis of any material assumptions/estimates.

Quality of accounting function

The quality of information provided by the finance department in a company will only be as good as the people preparing it. If the quality of staff within a department is sub-standard the information they generate will also be sub-standard. Directors must ensure that they are being properly served by their accounting function. To do this they will use their own judgement to assess the way the accounts have been put together, whether the accounts reflect their perception of how the company is performing, whether the finance staff are able to answer their questions about the accounts, the relationship between management and the financial staff throughout the company, any history of errors in information provided by the accounting function, and finally consider any comments that the auditors might have given to the directors concerning the general competence of the finance staff, for example in the letter written to the board concerning internal controls and other matters arising from their audit.

Directors' understanding

The purpose of management accounting information is to enable the company's management to assess the company's performance in previous periods and to make considered judgements concerning the future. The management accounts presented to the board must, therefore, be in a form which the directors are easily able to understand. The exact form of these accounts will not only depend on the nature of the business being reported but it will also depend on the degree of financial expertise of the directors. A director with considerable previous financial experience would almost certainly prefer a relatively detailed set of management accounts so that he could perform any detailed analysis he considered appropriate. In practice it is likely that at least half the board of directors, including a number of the independents may well not be experienced in accounting. It is therefore essential that the management information is provided in a clear concise form that is easily understood by all the directors. Supplementary information may be supplied for those who wish to receive it. It is desirable that at least one non-executive director is fairly well versed in accounting matters to ensure that there is an awareness among the independent directors of any creative accounting techniques that may have been used by the company's management.

An independent director who is fully aware of the limitations inherent in accounting information is well placed to make good use of that information.

Review of financial information: general approach

The remainder of this chapter considers each of the types of financial information that are available to the independent director and outlines some of the issues he should consider when examining them. The exact scope of the independent director's role will vary from company to company and will depend on many factors. As a minimum he should ensure that he performs his duties as a director, but there may be situations where the scope of his role would be considerably extended, for example, where a company is in financial difficulty and the board ask him to investigate the financial affairs of the company.

As a general rule, whatever the financial information being reviewed by an independent director, his basic objectives will be the same. He will want to satisfy himself that it is properly prepared, and then interpret/understand the content and finally make a decision or a series of decisions based on his findings. The structure of such a review will broadly be:

Stage 1

Is the information properly prepared? Is it

- complete?
- accurate?
- timely?
- prepared on an appropriate basis (i.e. accounting policies etc)?
- consistent (with periods and with the budget) in its preparation?

Stage 2

Interpretation

- consider findings of stage 1.
- basic ratio analysis.
- review profit and loss account.
- review balance sheet.
- review cash flow statement.
- other.

Stage 3

Decisions.

Review of management accounts

Basis of preparation

Before analysing the content of management accounts an independent director should first consider whether the accounts have been properly prepared. He should consider:

- Have the accounts been prepared on a consistent basis with previous periods and the budgets with which they are compared?
- Have they proved accurate in the past, for example have there been significant differences between 12-months management accounts and the audited financial statements?
- What is the source of the data used to prepare the accounts? Are actual figures taken from the ledgers or are estimates used or a combination of both?
- Where estimates are made are they credible and consistent with what was originally budgeted for the period and with the director's perception of what has actually happened?
- Is the information sufficiently up to date to be of any use?

While it is clearly not reasonable to suggest that these questions are raised each time a set of management accounts is reviewed, the independent director should ensure that he makes an initial assessment of the overall standard of preparation of the management accounts at the time he joins the board and then reconsiders their quality from time to time (but at least once every 12 months).

There are no strict rules concerning the level of detail in which an independent director should review a set of management accounts. In practice it will range from a relatively rudimentary review of the figures to detailed in-depth analysis depending on the circumstances. One of the most common methods of analysing a set of accounts is ratio analysis.

Ratio analysis

A cold examination of accounts, using a few simple ratios, can be extremely helpful in analysing a company's accounts.

The numerical values of some ratios mean little when comparing one company to another yet they can be extremely useful in analysing the performance of a company from one period to another.

Gross margin: $\dfrac{\text{Gross profit}}{\text{Sales}}$

Gives a measure of the profitability of products before taking overheads into account. Small fluctuations can indicate large changes in performance.

Operating margin: $\dfrac{\text{Operating profit}}{\text{Sales}}$

A measure of the profitability of the business after overheads but before interest, investment income or financing costs.

Interest cover: $\dfrac{\text{Operating profit}}{\text{Net interest charge}}$

A measure of the company's ability to fund its financing costs. A figure of less than one indicates that the company is unable to fund its interest charge out of current period profits. A figure between one and two should also be of some concern as interest charges still represent a significant proportion of profits.

Dividend cover: $\dfrac{\text{Earnings per ordinary share}}{\text{Dividends per ordinary share}}$

If dividend cover is greater than or equal to one then the company is able to pay the dividends out of profits or ordinary activities in the period. If less than one the company will either be paying it out of reserves or extraordinary profits. It is a crude measure of the company's ability to sustain the current level of dividends in future periods.

Gearing: $\dfrac{\text{Net borrowing}}{\text{Shareholders' funds}}$

Gearing is the extent to which the business is funded by borrowings relative to equity. A high gearing ratio is generally considered to represent higher levels of risk. An increase in gearing can be a cause for concern.

Earnings per share (EPS):The profit after tax, minority interests and preference dividends but before extraordinary items per equity share ranking for dividend in the period.

EPS is one of the most common measures used by analysts to measure the performance of a share (see also price earnings ratio).

Price earnings ratio:

$$\frac{\text{Share price}}{\text{Earnings per share}}$$

Not strictly a measure of the performance of the company but rather an indication of the market's perception of the quality of the company. Comparison of the price earnings (p/e) ratio between two different types of business is of limited value but the comparison of p/e ratios between two similar businesses can be very interesting. A higher p/e ratio can indicate: high quality earnings (i.e. low risk), large established business, out performing competitors in future periods, expected bids for the company and so on.

Quick ratio:

$$\frac{\text{Current assets} - \text{stock}}{\text{Current liabilities}}$$

Current ratio:

$$\frac{\text{Current assets}}{\text{Current liabilities}}$$

Both measures of the short-term funding of the company.

Debtor days:

$$\frac{\text{Trade debtors}}{\text{Turnover in period}} \times \text{number of days in period}$$

A measure of how long, on average, the company's trade debtors take to settle their debts. An increase in this figure can indicate problems, for example poor collection procedures, unidentified bad debts, a general slow down in payments etc. A very useful management statistic.

Stock turnover: $$\frac{\text{Stock}}{\text{Cost of sales for period}} \times \text{number of days in period}$$

A measure of how long, on average, items remain in stock. An increase in this figure can indicate problems, for example poor stock control, obsolete stock, overstocking perhaps caused by falling sales, error etc. Again a useful management statistic.

Profit and loss account

Under normal circumstances a non-executive director should focus his attention on the key performance indicators in the profit and loss account, looking at trends and comparing performance with previous periods and the budget.

Sales

The income companies generate from the sales of their products or services is clearly the most important feature of the business. Any failure to achieve budgeted levels of income may result in a drastic effect on the company's profitability and cash flow. This will be particularly true for companies with relatively high fixed over-heads and relatively low direct costs of sales. The following should be considered:

- Have sales volumes been achieved?
- Has product mix varied?
- Have prices changed?

Comparison should be made with budget and comparable prior period performance. Both favourable and adverse changes in the above may require investigation. The knock-on effect of any changes should also be considered, for example:

- Should stock levels and/or production volumes be increased or decreased?
- Should the marketing strategy be altered?
- What are the cash flow implications?

Gross margin

Gross margin is the profit a business generates directly from the sale of its products. The gross margin must exceed the company's overheads and financing costs if the company is to make a profit. When looking at gross margin consideration should be given not only to the monetary value of that margin but also to the percentage of the margin in relation to sales. Again, explanations should be sought for variations in the gross margin, both in terms of percentage and value. An increase/decrease in gross profit value may be due to any of the following respectively:

• higher/lower volumes.
• higher/lower selling prices.
• lower/higher costs of sales.
• error!

Examination of the gross profit percentage (GP%) will help to shed further light on movements in gross margin value:

• GP% up: suggests selling price has risen or cost of sales has fallen relative to the other.
• GP% down: suggests selling price has fallen or cost of sales has risen relative to the other.
• GP% same: selling prices have remained at a constant mark-up on cost.

Overheads

It is essential that very close attention is given to overheads. For each type of overhead the non-executive director should consider:

• comparison with budget and prior periods.
• whether the expenditure is necessary in the context of the current level of activity of the business.
• whether the capacity of the company to meet future operational targets could be restricted by the current overhead structure.

In practice, the most likely problem to arise is a loss of control over such expenditure which is particularly serious where a company is also failing to meet trading targets.

In a situation where the company is not achieving budgeted gross profit, the overhead budgets may need to be reconsidered and it may be appropriate to consider the possibility of reducing overhead expenditure. This could take the form of redundancies, or movement of non-essential staff from central city locations to regional locations, or perhaps the reduction of a high advertising expenditure budget.

Financing costs

The profit and loss account only provides part of the picture so far as the financing costs of a business are concerned. It will have to be read in conjunction with the balance sheet and cashflow statement. Any significant increase in financing cost or reduction in financing income should put a non-executive director on guard as to potential future problems with cash. He should consider:

- comparison with budget and prior periods.
- whether it is reasonable in the context of the relevant balance sheet assets and liabilities (i.e. investments, deposits and borrowings).
- whether the costs are being managed effectively. Is the best rate of interest being paid/received? Why is the company paying interest when it has an amount on deposit?
- how exposed the company is to interest rate fluctuations.

Balance sheet

The balance sheet will provide little information about the performance of the company in a period. It does, however, provide an indication of a company's financial position at the end of a period, i.e. at the date of the balance sheet.

Net assets

A balance sheet does not necessarily reflect all the assets of an enterprise (for example certain goodwill). However, the net assets of the business may give some useful information about the financial solidity of an enterprise as will the movement since the last balance sheet.

Net current assets

This figure gives an indication of a company's liquidity. Net current liabilities are a particular cause for concern as it could indicate insufficient funds to continue trading.

In this situation particular attention should be given to the cash flow position of the company.

Gearing

The extent to which a company is geared is also readily apparent from a balance sheet.

Cash flow statements

The survival of a business depends on it having sufficient funds to meet its liabilities as they fall due. It is, therefore, essential that management remains in control of the cash position at all times. Cash flow statements typically show the net opening cash position, the movements in the period and the closing position. This is then compared with budget and with available bank facilities.

Headroom

Headroom is the amount by which the borrowing facilities a company has negotiated exceed its actual borrowings. If he identifies low headroom an independent director should raise the matter with the board to ensure that steps are being taken either to reduce borrowings or increase facilities.

Cash flows in the period

Sales receipts, payments to creditors, payroll and capital expenditure are likely to be the major cash flows in the period. These should be reviewed and compared with budgets and variances investigated. Taxation cash flows can impact seriously on the cash position, particularly corporation tax where the current year's payment relates to the previous year's profits.

Facilities

Facilities should be negotiated at least six months and preferably twelve months ahead.

Other matters

Contingent liabilities

A major potential area of risk for a company that would not actually be reflected in accounting figures is that of contingent liabilities. A company should maintain a full register of all claims, or potential claims, that might be made against the company. Such a record would normally be kept by a company secretary and should be available for examination at all board meetings. The major items should be discussed in some detail. A non-executive director will wish to satisfy himself that not only is the company maintaining a proper record of such contingencies, but also that it is obtaining adequate legal advice on each significant claim. Additionally, some contingent liabilities will change into actual liabilities. It is sometimes difficult to determine the point of change, but when it happens, then it should be reflected as a cost in the profit and loss account and the cash flow projections.

Off balance sheet finance

The benefit of off balance sheet finance is quite literally that it does not appear on the balance sheet. For example, in the case of an operating lease for which the company is permitted to pay rentals for five years there is no disclosure in the balance sheet whatsoever. A rental charge for the year will be disclosed in the notes to the profit and loss account and disclosure of the commitment will be made in the notes to the balance sheet. As the operating lease is disclosed in none of the primary financial statements there is a possibility that it will be overlooked in a quick examination of the accounts. Increasingly directors are becoming more aware of the potential benefits to them (and not necessarily to their shareholders) of more sophisticated off balance sheet measures. The independent director should discuss with the board such matters as operating leases, quasi-subsidiaries, sale and leaseback agreements, and any other capital or rental commitments the company might have entered into.

The area of off balance sheet finance is relatively complex and the average independent director cannot expect to be an expert. It may therefore be that if his suspicion is aroused he might wish to commission a special report on the subject.

Creative accounting

Creative accounting by its nature is extremely hard to detect. The exponents of the art are taking advantages of others' limitations in interpretation of such treatments together with loopholes in current standard accounting and company law practice. Typical examples of where creative accounting might be used are:

- off balance sheets schemes.
- fair valuing in the context of acquisition accounting.
- profits moving, unusual interpretations of SSAP 24 for dealing with pension surpluses.
- liberal interpretation of SSAP 6 (extraordinary items).
- unusual revenue recognition policies.
- sale and leaseback agreements.
- foreign currency manipulation.
- changing the basis of accounting estimates, particularly bad debt and stock obsolescence provisions.

Review of budgets

When a budget is presented to the board the independent director will need to satisfy himself that it forms a credible basis for management decisions. There are, however, a number of issues he should consider to ensure that it is prepared on a reasonable basis:

- Is it prepared on a consistent basis with previous budgets and management accounts?
- How accurate have previous budgets proved to be?
- Is the budget a full-scale zero based budget or simply last year's figures adjusted?
- What are the major assumptions and are they reasonable?
- Are the profit and loss budget, the budgeted balance sheets and the budgeted cash flow statement integrated, or were they separately prepared?

If he is satisfied with the overall basis of preparation of the budget he should then go on to consider the figures themselves. The level of detail he decides to go into will depend on many factors including: his perception of the quality of management and the budgeting process; the financial position of the company; the significance of the budget for decision-making purposes; and his agreed time commitment to the company.

For predictive and decision-making purposes the most important elements of a budget are the profit and loss account and working capital/cash flow statements. The independent director might consider the following.

Profit and loss account

- Trend analysis: comparison of sales, margins, expenses and profits with previous years and previous budgets for the same period.
- Assumptions
  Turnover: reasons for changes from last year, pattern of sales, evidence for change in volume, effect of price changes, effect of price on volume in previous years, level of discounts.
  Production capacity: can existing capacity meet forecast requirements, can sufficient supplies be purchased, is sufficient trained labour available?
  Cost of production: has account been taken of wage rises,

materials and overhead price rises, maintenance costs and
new plant/start up costs?
Other costs and credits: has adequate provision been made for
stock losses, advertising and other costs?
Interest: based on bank's estimated rate and cash forecast
foreign currency assumptions including hedging
taxation.

- Accounting policies: are they consistent and acceptable?
- Calculations: have they been checked?
- Sensitivity analysis: have the main areas of vulnerability been
identified and sensitivity analysis been done? Are there any
contingencies built into the forecast?
- Does the budget make sense?

Working capital budget

- Is the working capital budget fully integrated with the
company's profit and loss account budget?
- Is the starting point a reliable balance sheet?
- Assumptions
  Trade creditors: are payments forecast on the basis of credit
  period, expected trading levels, margins, stock levels and
  inflationary effects?
  Other costs: are forecast payments based on credit periods
  and expected costs?
  Remittances: are they based on reasonable customer credit
  periods, expected bad debts, forecast sales and inflation?
  Stock: are levels based on forecast trading, seasonal fluctua-
  tion and inflation?
  VAT and PAYE: timing, amount.
  Taxation/dividends: timing, amount
  other capital items: redemptions, share issues etc.
- Calculation
- Borrowing limits: how do the forecasts compare? How far
ahead have they been agreed?
- Sensitivity analysis: as above.
- Conclusion

Capital expenditure

- Commercial viability: has each item been justified on a commercial basis?
- Can we afford it?
- Does it tie into the cash flow/working capital forecasts?

Review of statutory accounts

The annual financial statements of a company are not intended to be an internal management tool but rather a report to shareholders on the stewardship of the directors of the company over its assets and trade. The trading performance of the company during the period covered by the report should already have been communicated to the directors via the management accounts.

As a minimum the non-executive director should:

- Read and digest the full contents of the annual report to ensure that:

    He agrees with its contents, and
    nothing significant has been omitted.

- Satisfy himself that he understands all the material differences between the financial statements and the management accounts and why they have occurred. (Note: if they arise from matters found by the auditors, or significant final adjustments indicated by management, then doubt is thrown on the credibility of the management accounts as they were built up over the year.)
- Ensure that the auditors' opinion on the financial statements is not going to be qualified, and if it is, understand why.
- Ensure that preparing the financial statements on a going concern basis is appropriate.
- Ensure that any contingencies have been properly recorded.

The overriding consideration for the directors should be that they have a legal responsibility for the financial statements and that they are likely to be used by third parties as well as shareholders.

Danger signals

There are many ways in which a non-executive director can identify that all may not be well in a company. Some of the signals are related to financial and accounting matters and others are of a more general nature. A recent review of the characteristics of listed companies that have gone into liquidation or receivership has shown that certain key characteristics are portrayed by many of these enterprises. Features that they had in common were:

- The Chairman is also the chief executive or managing director.
- The gearing is more than 100%.
- The gearing has increased significantly over the last year.
- Short-term borrowings are in excess of long-term borrowings.
- Turnover has grown at more than 50% per annum over the last five years.
- Turnover has doubled since last year.
- The company has made or is planning to make a move of premises.
- Directors have resigned over the last year.
- The company is in a cyclical industry.
- The report and accounts are rather lavish and of a non-standard shape or size!.

The research warned that if a company had any more than five of the above characteristics then it was in a potential risk position, if it had more than eight an investor should only invest in such a company after checking it out thoroughly. Other characteristics of risk companies mentioned by the report include:

- The company indulges in creative accounting.
- The company is expanding rapidly and aggressively.
- The non-executive director identifies board room friction in the meetings.
- The company has a number of off balance sheet finance schemes.
- The company has indulged in a great deal of acquisition accounting.
- As part of that acquisition accounting it is indulged in a high

degree of fair value accounting, in particular in relation to reorganization provisions.
- Certain sectors, for example property, are higher risk than others.
- The company is listed on the USM.

In addition to highlighting the general danger signals some of the common accounting and financial signals that would indicate that a company might be in some difficulty are:

- Profit and loss account
    falling sales volumes or prices
    falling gross margin
    escalating overheads
    excessive interest charges
    losses.
- Balance sheet
    negative reserves
    net current liabilities.
- Working capital
    negative working capital
    forecast net cash outflows
    proximity to overdraft limits
    facilities for renewal.

Financial difficulty

If a director thinks that the company is in financial difficulty he should, together with his co-directors, *seek and obtain professional advice*. In the first instance, the company's auditors should be able to help. In practice, unless the financial difficulties have arisen suddenly, they would be aware of the company's situation as they carry out a review as part of their normal auditing procedures.

Depending on the advice given to the directors by the auditors, the directors may take any of the following courses of action:

- Commission an investigation into the current financial position of the company and develop a recovery plan. This might be carried out by employees of the company or by the auditors or by both.

- Seek and obtain the advice of a 'licensed insolvency practitioner' who specializes in administrations, receiverships or liquidations. This need not necessarily lead to the liquidation of the company.
- Decide that internal discussion and investigation should be sufficient to rectify matters.

In any event, it is important that the company's bankers are kept well informed of the situation. Frequently, financial difficulties arise because of temporary cash flow problems. However, a well-presented case to the bank, supported by the company's professional advisers, may enable a company to obtain an increased loan facility. Depending on the circumstances, it may be advisable for the company's creditors to be contacted to defer payments of outstanding amounts.

The alternatives

First, before any informed decision can be made about the company's future the directors are likely to be advised to ensure that the accounting records are up to date and regular management accounts are prepared. Frequently, when companies experience financial difficulties, administrative factors are neglected in favour of what happens at the 'sharp end'. One of the first considerations, if the company is experiencing cash flow problems, will be to produce short-term profit forecasts and cash flow projections. In the long term, it may be necessary to ascertain the parts of a business' activities that are profitable and those that are not and to consider whether businesses should be sold, terminated or re-organized.

Second, it may be that, after investigating the financial position of the company thoroughly, the directors conclude that it is insolvent and cannot trade its way out of the situation. There are many options that may be taken. It is not practicable to give more than an outline of these here, but the following may be of assistance in understanding the proposals that might be put forward by professional advisers. Some of these opinions are commercial in nature, others relate to the procedures established for insolvent companies by law. Not all of these relate to the winding up of a company. The law was sweepingly revised in the Insolvency Act 1986 and the procedures established there provide a framework in which ailing companies may be able to survive. The order in which the options are laid out commences with those which will least affect the company and end with the compulsory termination of the company's life. The options are:

- An injection of capital.
- Arrangements with creditors.
- Reconstruction or amalgamation.
- An 'administration order'.
- Receivership.
- Voluntary winding-up.
- Compulsory winding-up.

Penalties for continuing to trade unlawfully

If the directors continue to trade they may be at risk. The law provides five principal sanctions against directors who, in dealing with the company's assets, act irresponsibly with regard to its creditors.

- Criminal liability for fraudulent trading.
- Personal liability for fraudulent trading.
- Personal liability for wrongful trading.
- Misfeasance.
- Disqualification.

Review of current working capital position

The most common form of financial difficulty faced by companies is a deficiency in working capital. Set out below is a guide to the steps that might be taken when evaluating a company's working capital position.

Possible causes

There are many reasons why a company may be experiencing problems with working capital. These include:

- Internal management/administration problems.
- Short-term requirements for additional working capital.
- Poor collection from essentially good debtors, for example customers financing themselves at suppliers' expense.
- Significant bad debts.
- Poor forecasting leading to failure to negotiate adequate facilities with banks.
- Major capital expenditure projects drawing short term funds out of the business.
- Inherent lack of profitability.

Before management can hope to improve matters they must first identify the cause. In some cases the company may have sufficient expertise among its employees to identify the problems but, in most circumstances, external advice should be sought.

Stocks

In many companies the control of stock is of paramount importance, and can be a significant drain on working capital. Any company with stock should, as a minimum, have the following controls:

- Effective planning procedures to ensure that excessive stock is not held, while ensuring that demand can be met. This is particularly important in cyclical industries where high stock levels need only be maintained at certain times in the year.
- Physical controls to ensure that stock does not simply walk out of the warehouse unrecorded.
- Regular stocktakes to ensure that the book value of stock reflects what is physically held.
- Procedures to identify damaged, slow moving and obsolete stock and to ensure that they are not overvalued.

Failure to apply any of the first three controls could lead to a deterioration in the working capital position.

A high level review of stock would include:

- Compare with prior year, prior month and budget

  - value
  - stock turnover (number of days sales held in stock)

  An increase in either could indicate a drain on working capital.
- Review of most recent stocktake

  - how recent?
  - what were the findings?

  Does this suggest either an unreliable accounting system or lack of physical controls over the assets?
- Discussion of stock re-ordering policy with relevant management. Is it

  - based on expected demand?
  - phased?
  - regularly updated to reflect actual demand?
  - are orders tendered to ensure optimum price?
  - have any sales been lost due to stock-outs?

- Examine age analysis of stocks held.

  - are provisions made where necessary?
  - how did these problems arise?
  - could slow moving/old stock be sensibly sold (albeit at low
  - profit or even a loss) to release working capital?

At the conclusion of this review it should be possible to establish whether a problem exists in this area and whether further action is required.

Debtors

The majority of many companies' sales will not be for cash. Invoices are raised to customers, debtors created and hopefully payment received in accordance with the company's terms of credit. The controls which one would expect to see over debtors include:

- Credit review of potential customers before they are given credit and effective credit limits on their accounts.
- Regular reminders to debtors whose balances are overdue.
- Regular review of age debt analysis to identify potential bad debts.
- Tight controls over credit notes, discounts and cash receipts.

A high level review of trade debtors would include:

- Comparison with prior year, prior month and budget of:

  – value (gross and after provisions)
  – debtor days (number of days sales in debtors, see below).

  An increase in either could indicate a drain on working capital.
- Review of age debt analysis to ensure that provisioning is adequate.
- Comparison of credit taken with credit terms.
- Volume of credit notes raised in period and comparison with prior periods.

A high level review of other debtors would involve:

- Comparison with prior periods and budget.
- General review for reasonableness, in particular ageing.

Debtor days

The debtor-days ratio as outlined above is a key indicator of the performance of the company both in relation to debt collection and in relation to the ability of customers to pay. A significant increase in debtor days can therefore either indicate poor internal management or indicate a problem with the customers in terms of payment.

If the problems with debt collection are internal the independent director should consider whether the problem is related to poor staff or whether it is a systems problem. Clearly, if an individual is good at collecting debts but does not have the information to tell him which debts are due he will be unable to perform his job effectively. On the other hand, if he does have that information and is unable to collect the debt then either he is not competent at his job and therefore should either be trained or replaced, or the customer is in financial difficulty or delaying payment for some other reason.

Where one or several customers are in financial difficulty it will be of some concern, particularly where major customers are involved. The independent director should question the executive directors of the company to ensure that they are both on top of the problem and actually doing something about it.

An ever-increasing debtor-days figure is a symptom of the failure to recognize bad debts. The non-executive should therefore also question the other executive directors on the company's policy towards the recognition of bad debts.

Cash and bank accounts

It is the cash deposit and current accounts, which are the most readily realizable source of assets for the company, that provide the day to day cash to run the business and require the most rigorous control. The key controls over cash are:

- Payments should be properly authorized
- Regular reconciliations of bank statements to cash book/ nominal ledger, independent review of reconciliations, and timely follow-up of reconciling items.
- Monitoring of borrowings against agreed facilities.

A high level review of bank balances would include:

- Comparison with prior periods and budget.
- Examination of above controls to ensure that they are in existence.
- Review of balances held on non-interest-bearing accounts and other balances to ensure that interest costs are minimized and where there is net interest income that it is maximized.
- Consider whether agreed facilities are adequate in the short, medium and longer term.

Creditors

The final significant element of working capital is the company's creditors. The fundamental controls over creditors include:

- Control over orders: authorization prior to placing, justification for expenditure, check to ensure included in budget.
- Control over suppliers: only use vetted suppliers, special approval for non-standard suppliers.
- Control over payments: proper approval of payments – only pay on approved invoices and independent cheque signatories.

A high-level review of trade creditors would include:

- Comparison with prior periods and budget.
- Consideration in the context of profit and loss account charges to ensure that the level of creditors is reasonable.
- Ensure that the company is taking the suppliers' normal trade credit terms. If they are not, determine why not? Is there any scope for deferring payment on any large amounts?

A high-level review of other creditors would include:

- Comparison with prior periods and budget.
- General review for reasonableness, in particular unusual balances.

Conclusion

In summary, the level and depth in which the independent director will examine a company's accounting position will depend on the circumstances. In a healthy company where the non-executive director has no reason to believe that there are any significant problems he would normally focus on the basics. As a minimum he should perform a high-level review of the following:

- Management accounts – normally monthly

    profit and loss account
    balance sheet

cash flow statement
key ratios (debtor days, stock turnover, interest cover)
bank facilities
legal commitments.

- Six monthly/annually

  budget (in some detail)
  results of stocktake
  annual report/six-month results.

- Ad hoc reports

  potential acquisitions
  potential disposals
  specifically commissioned reviews.

In a healthy company an independent director should be able to satisfy himself at the board meeting about any matter he wishes to raise in relation to the above and there his responsibility would rest. However, there will be instances where there are problems, either that the independent director identifies following his reviews or, more likely, that are brought to his attention by executive directors on the board. Such problems would normally be resolved through detailed discussion with senior management of the company. In the unlikely event that the executive directors are not able to satisfy the independent directors that they are managing the company efficiently and in the best interests of the shareholders, the independent directors will have to consider their position. At this point they should analyse the information they are given at the board meeting in as much detail as possible. First they should examine each division of the company in detail in the way that they would normally examine the company as a whole. This may enable them to pinpoint more accurately where the trouble is actually occurring. The non-executive should then seek further information from that particular division. In the event that the director does not have sufficient time or expertise to examine the problem himself he must consider commissioning an independent report.

8

Directors' disqualification and insurance

Section 1: Disqualification of directors under the Company Directors Disqualification Act 1986

David Allen and Ian McDonald
Rowe and Mawr Solicitors

Register of disqualified directors

Disqualification orders made under the 1986 Act are now included on the register of disqualified persons kept under previous legislation. The register is maintained at the Companies Registration Offices in Cardiff, London and Edinburgh. No fee is currently payable for inspection of the register.

All references to statutory provisions in this chapter are to sections of the Company Directors Disqualification Act 1986 unless otherwise specified.

The statements made in this chapter are believed to be an accurate summary of the law as at 31 October, 1991.

Introduction

This chapter primarily deals with the provisions of the Company Directors Disqualification Act 1986 which set out the circumstances in which orders may be made disqualifying persons from acting as company directors. It does not deal with other statutory provisions found, for example, in the Companies Act 1985 and The Pluralities Act 1838 which also place restrictions on those eligible to be directors.

The 1986 Act consolidates changes which were brought into effect initially on 28 April 1986 in the Insolvency Act 1985 on the recommendation of the Cork Committee. While it was recognized that limited liability companies and the protection of directors from personal liability was to be encouraged so as to enable directors to take risks in the pursuance of the generation of wealth, it was considered that an end must be brought to the fraudulent practices that this aim engendered. This practice was most evident in the time-honoured formula consisting of the formation of companies, the running up of debts, the milking of assets followed by the liquidation of the company; a process which could be carried on ad infinitum.

The Act in no way restricts existing common law remedies available against a director, for example for breach of the duty of the director of an insolvent company to act to protect the interests of creditors. Instead, the Act sets out some of the factors which a court will take into account when considering whether a disqualification order should be made. These factors have been further expanded by recent case law. The Act also stipulates against whom an order can be made and by whom it may be sought, the maximum, and in one case minimum, duration of an order and the consequences of its breach.

The Act applies to companies which may be wound up under the Insolvency Act 1986, and therefore applies both to registered and unregistered companies. Directors, de facto directors or shadow directors of unregistered companies may also, therefore, be liable for wrongful or fraudulent trading. The provisions of section 11 dealing with undischarged bankrupts apply both to unregistered companies and to companies incorporated outside Great Britain which have an established place of business in Great Britain.

Since 1987, more than 1,000 disqualification orders have been made and at the end of June 1991 a further 699 applications were pending. The number of orders made in 1991 is expected to be double that made in 1990.

Shadow directors

A 'shadow director' is defined in Section 22(5) as being, 'a person in accordance with whose directions or instructions the directors of the company are accustomed to act (but so that a person is not deemed a shadow director by reason only that the directors act on advice given by him in a professional capacity).'

It will be seen that a number of the provisions are drafted specifically to catch shadow directors. In particular they are caught by the provisions relating to unfitness and wrongful and fraudulent trading. The definition is very far-reaching, and is designed to catch not only appointed officers but also those who 'pull the strings'. For example, a bank may be deemed to be a shadow director if it gives directions or instructions rather than professional advice. Similarly, a holding company may be a shadow director where it exercises a degree of control over the decision-making of the board of one of its subsidiaries.

In a recent case, Mr Justice Vinelott refused to strike out an application seeking a disqualification order against a management consultant who had been installed by a major investor in a company to advise and assist in the recovery of its business. It was stated that such a person may well have become a de facto or shadow director and hence susceptible to the provisions of the 1986 Act. In a previous case it was held that the terms 'management consultant' and 'company doctor' have no legal significance.

The provisions of the Insolvency Act 1986 and the Company Directors Disqualification Act apply to anyone occupying the position of director whatever his or her job title may be. The provisions therefore cover those who are directors in substance as well as those validly in office.

The effect of a disqualification order (Section 1)

If an order is made against a person he may not, without leave of the court, be a director of a company, a liquidator or administrator of a company, a receiver or manager of a company's property, or be 'in any way, whether directly or indirectly, concerned or take part in the promotion, formation or management of a company, for a specified period beginning with the date of the order'. The court has said of this definition that, 'it would be difficult to imagine a more comprehensive phraseology designed to make it impossible for persons to be part of the management and central direction of company affairs'.

Where more than one order is made against a person, the periods of disqualification run concurrently.

Grounds for disqualification

Disqualification for general misconduct in connection with - companies

1 Disqualification on conviction of indictable offence (Section 2)

An order may be made if a person is convicted of an indictable offence (whether the conviction is made on indictment or summarily) in connection with the promotion, formation, management or liquidation of a company or the receivership or management of its property. An example of such an offence is fraud.

This ground is extremely broad. A management consultant acting as adviser to the board of a company has been held to be acting in connection with the management of the company. The offence is not limited to the internal management of the company's affairs. For example, an order has been made against a director who set fire to his company's premises in an attempt to claim the insurance. An order has also been made against a director fraudulently raising finance from third parties.

The maximum period of disqualification for an offence under this section is five years if convicted by a court of summary jurisdiction (for example a Magistrates court) and fifteen years in any other case. In considering what term of disqualification to apply, the court may consider the director's age and the unlikelihood of him finding other employment but will also consider the number of offences committed and the sum of money involved.

2 Disqualification for persistent breaches of companies legislation (Section 3)

It is often the case that insolvent companies have failed to observe statutory obligations to keep proper accounting records or return audited accounts. Section 3 is broader than the previous legislation which required three previous *convictions* for default before an order could be made. It is now only necessary for a director to be 'persistently in default'. Three or more defaults in the five-year period prior to the application is conclusive proof of persistent default but an order may be made under this head even without three such offences.

A person is treated as guilty of a default if a default order is made against him for failure to deliver company accounts, to prepare revised accounts, to make returns, or in the case of a receiver, manager or liquidator, failure to make returns.

There is no need for it to be shown that there was an intention to flout the law, but such an intention will be taken into account by the court when considering the period of disqualification to apply. The court has indicated that it views persistent default in relation to formalities as a serious offence. The maximum period of disqualification under this section is five years.

In one case in which an order was made for the maximum five-year period, defaults in making returns were combined with insolvent trading and what amounted to theft from creditors. There were also substantial Crown debts.

A similar provision exists in section 5 which permits an order to be made at the same time that the final conviction for breach of filing requirements is made, provided that the director is found to be 'unfit' within the meaning of section 6.

3 Disqualification for fraud, etc. in winding up (Section 4)

This provision permits an order to be made if it appears that the director is guilty of fraudulent trading (see later) whether or not he has been convicted. There is no requirement that the company should be insolvent. This provision applies to, among others, shadow directors, liquidators and receivers.

The maximum period for an order under this section is fifteen years.

4 Disqualification for unfitness (Sections 6 and 7)

Disqualification under this heading is most common. Although 'unfitness' is not a new concept, the Act lists specific factors which will be taken into account and consequently it is now easier to make an order under this head.

Any misconduct can be relevant. The court should be satisfied that the director is guilty of one or more serious failures, whether deliberate or through incompetence. The court is concerned to see that the director is capable of performing 'those duties attendant on the privilege of conducting business' through companies with limited liability. Ordinary commercial misjudgement is seemingly not sufficient. A director must show 'lack of commercial probity', although it has been suggested by Browne-Wilkinson VC that, 'in an extreme case of gross negligence or total incompetence disqualification could be appropriate'.

On the other hand, it has been said that misfortune or misjudgement should not be equated with serious neglect meriting disqualification. Care will be taken not to judge a director's decisions with hindsight. A director should not, for example, be criticized for failing to realize that particularly favourable trading conditions were coming to an end.

One case illustrating this balancing approaching is that of *Re Bath Glass Ltd.* (1988) 4 BCC 130. The company in question was a craft products company formed in 1973, of which one director had been so for 15 years and another for 8 years when the company ceased trading in early 1986 and went into compulsory liquidation in July of that year. The criticism of the respondent directors were described in this manner by Mr Justice Peter Gibson:

'By the middle of 1982 Bath Glass was insolvent, its liabilities exceeding its assets. The position grew worse in the next two years as year after year forecasts and budgets were not achieved. [The respondents] knew that Bath Glass could only survive with the support of its bank, but that [the bank] could call in its debts at any time. They knew that, even with that banking support, they were in arrears with the payment of Crown debts, and that for a substantial period of time. They further knew that they were using amounts representing tax received from Collective [another company of which they were directors] to carry on business. In particular, they knew in the last six months of trading that the Crown debts were going unpaid and indeed increasing while the bank borrowings went down. There was an increasing risk that creditors would be left unpaid if the bank could not be persuaded to grant substantial overdraft facilities. In my judgment, that is improper conduct and a wrong way in which to conduct business. They must have known they were trading at the risk of creditors.'

While on the face of it this course of action appears to show the 'lack of commercial probity' described by Browne-Wilkinson VC (see earlier), the court looked at the conduct of the directors as a whole. In particular, Mr Justice Peter Gibson found that they had not been dishonest and had not acted with a view to benefiting themselves at the expense of creditors. The reduction of bank borrowing had been at the bank's insistence. By paying off the company's overdraft and taking shares in return, they showed a readiness to make a personal commitment to the company. The company forecasts which proved inaccurate had been prepared with care, the directors acted on professional advice and to a certain extent the company's misfortunes were beyond their control.

Mr Justice Peter Gibson concluded that although the directors' conduct had been 'imprudent and improper in part', it was not sufficiently serious for them to be considered unfit to be concerned in the management of a company.

The section applies not only to directors and former directors, but also to shadow directors. It has been held under the precursor to this section that a de facto director who acted as such without proper appointment is included within the scope of this provision.

For an order to be made, the director must be, or have been, a director or shadow director of a company which has at any time become insolvent. If this is the case, the director's conduct in relation to other companies which remain solvent will be considered, as will be his conduct with regard to any overseas companies of which he is also a director.

'Insolvent' has an artificial meaning for the purpose of this section. It includes a situation where an administration order has been made or where an administrative receiver has been appointed under a floating charge. It is therefore possible that a director will be disqualified for unfitness even though he has been associated with no company which has become insolvent in a business sense.

One of the most common reasons for disqualification for unfitness is failure to set aside sufficient funds to pay PAYE, National Insurance contributions and VAT, that money instead being used as working capital as insolvency looms.

The Act sets out a number of matters which will be considered in determining the unfitness of a director. These matters are relevant but not exhaustive. They are as follows:

i   Breach of fiduciary or any other duty by the director.
ii Misapplication or retention by the director of any money or other property of the company. The obligation to repay need not be that of the director. The director would still be caught by this provision if he had passed the property in question to his wife or a friend.
iii The extent of the director's responsibility for the company entering into a transaction which is liable to be set aside as a debt avoidance transaction.
iv The extent of the director's responsibility for failure to comply with filing formalities (see ii above). The specific matters referred to are:
   • company's duty to keep accounting records.
   • company's obligations with respect to place and length of time for keeping accounting records.
   • obligation of the company to keep and maintain a register of directors and secretaries of the company.
   • obligation of the company to keep and maintain a register of members of the company.
   • the company's duties in relation to the location of the register of its members.
   • the company's duty to make annual returns.

- the company's obligations regarding the time for completion of the annual return.
- the company's duty to deliver particulars of charges on its property.

v The extent of the director's responsibility for failure to prepare annual accounts or to sign the company's balance sheet.

In addition, the following factors will be taken into account, but only where the company has become insolvent. These may be summarized as follows:

i   The extent to which the director was responsible for the company becoming insolvent.

ii The extent of the director's responsibility for any failure by the company to supply any goods or services which have been paid for. This is aimed at protecting consumers who have paid for goods which have not been delivered (e.g. on mail order). In such instances the consumers would be unsecured creditors should the company go into liquidation.

iii The director's responsibility for the company entering into any transaction giving a preference.

iv Failure to comply with the duty to call a creditors' meeting in a creditors' voluntary winding up. This is designed to prevent the delay of the appointment of a creditors' nominee as liquidator for a period long enough to allow corporate assets to be disposed of in a way to defeat the creditors' rights.

v   Failure of the director to comply with any obligation relating to the company's statement of affairs in administration, administrative receivership, voluntary liquidation or compulsory liquidation or his duty to cooperate with the liquidator.

In a recent Court of Appeal case, *Re Sevenoaks Stationers (Retail) Ltd.* [1990] 3 WLR 1165, the first appeal against a disqualification order to reach the Court of Appeal, the Court endorsed the suggestion that a three-tier approach should be adopted in relation to the length of any disqualification under this section. Lord Justice Dillon found it surprising and disturbing that in the 18-month period ending in June 1990, many more disqualifications for more than five years had been imposed in County Courts than in the High Court. It seems unlikely that the cases brought in the High Court were significantly less serious than those in the County Court.

In an effort to produce guidelines which could be uniformally applied, he suggested that a period of 11–15 years should be reserved for second offenders; six to 10 years should be used for serious cases; and two to five years for less serious cases such as failure to pay over VAT and PAYE money to the tax authorities. However, while some judges have treated the Crown as an involuntary debtor which directors should take greater care to pay, others have treated the omission to pay as serious but not sufficiently serious to merit a disqualification order.

Failure to keep accounts or to have them audited and failure to make returns has been held to be 'gross incompetence' which might incur a four to six year suspension. The suggested minimum period of four years was reduced in one case to two years because the director relied on a chartered secretary appointed by him to deal with the paperwork. No dishonesty had been found in this case. The judge attempted to balance the director's blameworthiness against the mitigating factor of the secretary's appointment, but also considered the need to protect the public from the director's incompetence.

Reliance on budgets and forecasts, acting on professional advice, employing a finance director, an absence of dishonesty and successful management of other companies will all be taken into account in the director's favour in considering whether an order should be made, and if so for how long.

The minimum period of disqualification under this section is two years. This is the only minimum period of disqualification provided for by the Act. The maximum period is 15 years.

Conduct of the director during previous insolvencies in which he was involved will be taken into account. As Mr Justice Hoffmann commented in one case when disqualifying the director for five years, the director in question had 'learned little from his previous insolvencies except perhaps a certain cunning in dealing with suppliers and disposing of assets'.

Where a liquidator, administrator, administrative receiver or the Official Receiver feels that a director's conduct in a company with which he is dealing is unfit, he must report that to the Secretary of State who may then apply to the Court for a disqualification order. There is a duty on the liquidator, administrator or administrative receiver (as the case may be) to produce such books, papers and other records relevant to the person's conduct as a director to the Secretary of State. His report will include the conduct of directors, former directors and shadow directors. The application for a disqualification order must be made within two years from the day on which the company became insolvent.

Where a full report has not been submitted within six months of:

i   the liquidator's appointment; or
ii the liquidator forming the opinion that, at the time when the company went into liquidation, its assets were insufficient for the payment of its debts and other liabilities and the expenses of winding up; or
iii the administrative receiver's appointment; or
iv in the case of the administrator, the date of the administration order being made in relation to the company.

an interim report must be submitted to the Secretary of State. The insolvency practitioner is required in this report to state why no full report has been submitted. This might be because the company is solvent, because he has found no conduct falling within the 'unfitness' provisions of section 6, or because he has insufficient information.

As mentioned earlier, the insolvency practitioner is required to report on shadow directors as well as on directors. He must therefore decide whether or not a person falls within the definition of 'shadow director', as well as deciding whether or not a director is 'unfit'. Notes issued by the Department of Trade and Industry give guidance as to the approach which should be taken by the insolvency practitioner. These notes say:

'In forming a view of conduct which may be considered unfit, office holders [i.e. insolvency practitioners] are asked not to take a pedantic view of isolated technical failures, e.g. the occasional lapse in filing annual returns, etc, but to form an objective view of the director's conduct. It is also stressed that the office holder is required to consider matters of conduct on the basis of information acquired in the course of his normal duties and by reference to the books and records available to him and is not obliged to undertake investigations which he would not otherwise have considered it necessary to make.'

5 Disqualification after investigation of a company (Section 8)

An application may be made for an order where the Secretary of State considers it 'expedient in the public interest' from information received after an investigation carried out by an inspector appointed by him. The application may be made against a director, former director or a shadow director of the company.

A disqualification order will normally follow if the investigation was being carried out under Section 177 Financial Services Act 1986 against a director for contravention of the Insider Dealing Regulations.

Unlike an application under Section 6 for disqualification for unfitness, the director's conduct in relation to other companies cannot be taken into account under this head and there is no minimum period of disqualification. The maximum period is 15 years.

The same factors will be considered as under the Section 6 application but, since the company need not be insolvent, the factors relating only to insolvent companies may not be relevant.

Other cases of disqualification

1 Participation in wrongful trading (Section 10)

If during the winding up of a company the Court makes a declaration that a person is liable to contribute to the company's assets under Sections 213 or 214 Insolvency Act 1986 having been found guilty of fraudulent or wrongful trading, then the Court may make a disqualification order even if no one applies for it. The maximum period of such an order is 15 years.

A person is liable for wrongful trading if he is or has been a director of an insolvent company at a time when he knew or ought to have known that there was no reasonable prospect that the company would avoid becoming insolvent and where he failed to take every step which he ought to have taken to minimize potential loss to the company's creditors. The provision covers shadow directors and corporate directors. Insolvency for these purposes is where the assets of the company are insufficient to pay the debts and other liabilities and the expenses of the winding up.

The question of what the director ought to have known or concluded is to be judged objectively and a further element of objectivity is introduced by the 'reasonable prospect' requirement.

There is a statutory provision for relief under Section 214. If the Court is satisfied that after the relevant time that person took every step that a reasonably diligent person would have taken with a view to minimizing the potential loss to the company's creditors, it may not make a declaration and hence no disqualification order may be made under this head.

In deciding what steps the person took or ought to have taken, his actions should be measured by the standard of a reasonably diligent person having the general knowledge, skill and experience that can reasonably be expected of someone carrying out the same functions as those carried out by the director.

This part of the test is objective. However, the test is two-fold. The director must, in addition to the objective test, satisfy the subjective test that he met the standard of a reasonably diligent person having the general knowledge, skill and experience that the director in question actually has. Therefore, while a high-calibre director will be judged by his own standard, a director of less competence will be judged by the standard of the reasonably competent director.

A person is guilty of fraudulent trading if it appears during the winding up that he has knowingly been a party to the carrying on of any business with intent to defraud creditors (whether of the company or of any other person) or for any other fraudulent purpose.

In addition to the possibility of a disqualification order being made, the Companies Act 1985 provides for criminal sanction. In the case of a prosecution on indictment the sentence may be a term of imprisonment of up to seven years, a fine or both, while on a summary conviction the appropriate sentence will be a term of imprisonment of up to six months, a fine up to the statutory minimum, or both.

While fraudulent trading requires proof of fraudulent intent, wrongful trading is a more objective test and is therefore much more commonly alleged. While wrongful trading can only apply where the company is in insolvent liquidation, the criminal sanction for fraudulent trading applies whether or not a company is in liquidation. A further difference between the two is that while wrongful trading applies only to directors and shadow directors, fraudulent trading applies to anyone who has been a 'party' to the fraudulent trading.

2 Personal bankruptcy (Section 11)

Bankruptcy leads, in effect, to automatic disqualification from acting as a director. No court order is required.

It is an offence for an undischarged bankrupt to act as a director of, or directly or indirectly take part in the promotion, formation or management of a company unless he obtains the permission of the Court by which he was adjudged bankrupt.

The Official Receiver is duty bound to state his opposition to any application by a bankrupt to become a director if he considers the application to be against the public interest.

While there has been no English case on this point, a recent decision of the Court in Northern Ireland approved the approach by the Australian Court placing the onus firmly on the bankrupt to establish that his application is an exception to the general principle that it is a strong policy of law that bankrupts should not act as directors of companies. It is therefore likely to be extremely difficult for an undischarged bankrupt to become a company director.

3 Failure to pay under a County Court administration order (Section 12)

Under the County Courts Act 1984 a County Court can make an administration order where a debtor is unable to pay a judgment debt against him, provided that his entire indebtedness does not exceed £5,000. The grounds on which an order may be made are to be widened by The Courts and Legal Services Act to include debts other than judgment debts.

Where a Court is administering the estate of an insolvent individual and he fails to make a payment under the arrangement, the administration order will be replaced by an order that he should not act as a director for a specific period of up to two years and that he should not alone or jointly obtain credit above a certain sum nor enter into any transaction connected with any business without disclosing to the other party that he is under these disabilities.

It should, perhaps, be emphasized that this form of administration order is in no way connected with the administration provisions of the Insolvency Act 1986.

Consequences of the contravention of a disqualification order

1 Criminal liabilities

If tried on indictment, a person may be sentenced to a fine or up to two years in prison or a combination of the two. There is no maximum fine which may be imposed. If tried summarily, he may be sentenced to not more than six months in prison and/or a fine not exceeding the statutory maximum.

2 Company liabilities

Where a body corporate is acting in contravention of a disqualification order, any officer of the company implicated in the contravention or a person purporting to act in that capacity is liable. The company is also liable.

3 Personal liability for the company's debts where the person acts while disqualified

Where a person either acts in contravention of a disqualification order or acts on the instructions of a person whom he knows to be disqualified, that person will be jointly and severally liable with others similarly responsible, and the company itself, for all the relevant debts of the company. The relevant debts for the purposes of this provision are those incurred while he was involved in the management of the company or, as the case may be, while he acted or was willing to act on the instructions of a disqualified person.

A creditor of the company may take proceedings against one disqualified director for the entirety of the debt. The director will be obliged to pay but may then seek a contribution from the company or any other debtor. Clearly, the company's contribution will be worthless if it is insolvent.

Section 2: Indemnity insurance

Francis de Zulueta
Special Risk Services

Directors' and officers' liabilities

An important development during the last few years in the UK has been the dramatic increase in the number and size of proceedings brought by shareholders, creditors or other third parties seeking to hold directors and officers of companies personally liable for losses they have suffered.

The realization by directors that they have unlimited personal liability in relation to their 'wrongful acts' such as breach of statutory duty, neglect, error or omission, misleading statement or breach of warranty of authority, has led an increasing number of companies to secure adequate Directors' and Officers' (D & O) liability insurance cover. However, there are still many companies which have not yet fully understood the complexities of D & O liability.

Most directors and officers of companies are aware that they owe legal obligations to the companies on whose boards they serve, but only those who have been involved in litigation are aware of the significant costs which can arise (regardless of the director's ultimate liability or guilt) and the fact that civil damages awarded may be enormous.

The Companies Act and D & O insurance

In the UK, D & O insurance products have been slow to take off because opinion in the UK market was confused as to whether Section 310 of the Companies Act 1985 precluded a company from arranging insurance for its directors and officers. Some solicitors believed that it was illegal to buy D & O insurance if the individual directors and officers were not personally paying for the product. Others believed that it was perfectly legal. As a way of circum-navigating this difficulty many companies purchased D & O insurance with a 90%/10% split. The company was deemed to be paying for 90% of the cover and the directors deemed to be contributing 10%, thus making it a personal as well as a corporate cover.

The 1989 Companies Act amended Section 310 of the Companies Act 1985, permitting a company to buy and maintain insurance on behalf of its directors and officers against any liability which may attach in respect of any negligence, breach of duty or breach of trust of which they may be guilty in relation to the company.

However, the provisions of the 1989 Act are permissive only. Before a company buys D & O cover on behalf of its directors and officers it must ensure that it gives power in the Memorandum of Association to do so. Where necessary a company may have to amend its Memorandum of Association accordingly. The fact that such cover has been purchased or maintained by the company on behalf of the directors and officers must be included in a company's report and accounts.

Referral should be made to the accountants for clarification as to whether the purchase of D & O insurance by the company is a taxable benefit in kind, although the trend indicates that it probably is. The Inland Revenue has not yet made a firm ruling on this.

The permission given in the 1989 Act for a company to purchase D & O cover on behalf of its directors and other officers is limited to its current officers. It does not extend to the purchase of such insurance on behalf of individuals previously occupying such positions. It should be noted that most D & O liability policies cover not only current but also former directors and therefore there could be a problem here.

The other point to make, while discussing the fact that provisions of policies do not match up with the law, is that many D & O policies require that Assureds remain silent about whether or not they have a policy to prevent the attraction of unwelcome claims. This does not fit well with the requirement in the 1989 Companies Act to disclose such a policy, and it will not take too long before inventive lawyers begin scanning back through the last few years' Reports and Accounts to see whether or not a D & O policy has been taken out.

Policies available are normally written on a 12-months basis and are what is known as 'claims made', which means that the claim must be made during the currency of the policy, although it may be triggered by actions taken or omitted prior to the date of the inception of the policy. In other words, most of these policies are what is known as 'fully retroactive'.

Who is a director?

The Companies Act 1985 defined a director in Section 741 (i) as 'any person occupying the position of a director, by whatever name called'. This would naturally include all those whose names might appear on the records at Companies House.

However, it is not always clear who is a director. Companies may give the title to an individual as a courtesy title designed to impress customers, such as 'associate directors' or 'sales directors' who may not in fact have a seat on the board. In other cases an individual may be a director without the title. Alternatively, a company may describe its directors as 'governors' or 'trustees' without affecting their legal status as directors.

The Institute of Directors has attempted to provide some clarification by suggesting that the title 'Director of . . .' is generally accepted as implying that the holder of the title does not sit on the board, while '. . . Director' is usually taken to imply that he does. It is likely that the courts will look at the substance of the position rather than the title adopted (re Low-Line Limited (1988) 3WLR 26).

A 'non-executive' director is equally liable in law for a company's actions as full-time executive directors on the same board, regardless of any limitation in executive duties, hours of work or earnings.

The Insolvency Act 1986 defines 'a shadow director' as a 'person in accordance with whose directions and instructions the directors of the company are accustomed to act'. For the purposes of the definition a company can be a person. There is not a clear explanation of what this means, but in practice it would include a company or person whom the directors were in a habit of consulting ('accustomed'), who gave clear instructions to do something. To give an example, a bank could be deemed a shadow director if it had excessive involvement in the management of its borrower's affairs.

The most serious liability would be incurred if someone were a shadow director and was also found to have been involved in wrongful trading in connection with the business of a borrower who has gone into insolvent liquidation. Such a person could become liable for the company's debts and may be disqualified from acting as a director of any company for up to 15 years (Company Directors' Disqualification Act 1986). He may also be prevented from being involved in the promotion, formation, management or liquidation of any company, or with the receivership or management of any company's property.

Who is an officer?

The term 'officers' (Section 214 of the Companies Act 1989) requires comment. The position of officer does not appear to be defined by parliament in this context (the definition in the Companies Act 1989 being unhelpful), but it does seem clear that its use in terms of identifying those upon whom the heavy burden of potential personal liability may fall is to extend the range of potential defendants down the company hierarchy from nominal directors to senior management. The title would include a director, a manager or a secretary of a company.

Director's duties

So far as the duties of a director are concerned, some are laid down by statute, but many are found only in common law.

There are fiduciary duties (a concept originally borrowed in the eighteenth and nineteenth centuries from the Courts of Equity where Trustees were placed in a position of trust in respect of assets) and those of skill and care.

Fiduciary duty is the duty of good faith; an individual director must act in good faith in his dealings with or on behalf of the company and exercise the powers and fulfil the duties of his office honestly. A director's fiduciary duties include the duty not to act outside the powers conferred upon him by the shareholders not to commit the company to transactions prohibited either by statute or common law.

A company director must not commit the company to a

transaction outside its charter, i.e. not envisaged in the company's Memorandum of Association. Nowadays, of course, most companies' Memoranda and Articles of Association will be extremely broad and should encompass all areas of activity, but it should be noted that acting outside the Memorandum and Articles of Association can give rise to liability, because the ultra vires action may not be legally enforceable against the company.

One other fiduciary duty that can represent a difficulty for directors is that of avoiding a conflict between their personal interests and their duty to the company. Perhaps this is particularly true of non-executive directors or indeed venture capital groups.

The directors' fiduciary duties impose on them a largely negative obligation to do nothing which conflicts with the company's interests. But when they are acting in the company's interests they are also expected to exercise whatever skill they possess and reasonable care. This duty of skill and care is encapsulated in a fast moving and substantial body of law, the Law of Negligence.

Directors and officers may be held liable for negligence to third parties in addition to, or in substitution of, the company. There has been a recent case where some Lloyds brokers were held liable on exactly this point, but again most D & Os' liability policies will exclude the provision of professional services to third parties, as this liability is deemed to be better suited to a professional liability policy. However, professional liability policies are generally intended to protect the company against the consequences of acts of its employees, rather than protect the individual directors. This appears to be a gap.

Certainly claims for libel and slander, or indeed breach of warranty of authority often associated with mergers and acquisitions activity, can give rise to claims of this nature.

A director need not exhibit in the performance of his duty a greater degree of skill than may be generally reasonably expected from a person of his knowledge and experience (re City Equitable Fire Insurance Company (1925)). It would appear that the courts will construe professional qualifications, for example, as a natural flag for the greatest degree of knowledge and experience. Therefore, in the case of an insolvency a chartered accountant on the board will be more in the firing line than, for example, the marketing director.

Legislation

There is now a vast body of legislation and supplementary regulation concerning the conduct of a company's business affairs, whether the company is private or public. As a director, while a person cannot necessarily be expected to know the full details of all the legislation which may apply to a company, he should clearly have a general understanding of what statutes and regulations apply and the key areas of activity which they affect.

Legislation which covers director's duties includes the Company's Securities (Insider Dealing) Act 1985, the Company Director's Disqualification Act 1986, the Insolvency Act 1986, the Financial Services Act 1986 and the Companies Act 1989. The Companies Act 1985 contains many pitfalls for directors and, in fact, includes over 200 provisions whereby a director can incur fines or penalties for failing to carry out his prescribed duties. Legislation then ranges from those statutes which are generally applicable to almost every type of company – taxes, employment, health and safety – through to those which may apply as a result of the company's particular field of business activity – financial services, control of pollution, sale of goods, insurance. These statutes often impose personal liability on directors of companies found guilty of offences of non-compliance.

There are also duties imposed on particular types of company and business by varous regulatory authorities such as the Stock Exchange, the Takeover Panel and self-regulatory organizations such as IMRO and FIMBRA, and European legislation, which ultimately governs all UK legislation, will be increasing rather than decreasing directors' responsibilities.

The amount of legislation affecting directorial responsibility has been growing dramatically over the last few years and it is quite clear that the government intends to ensure that careless or even cowboy directors are punished for their lack of diligence and the abandonment of their duty of care to their shareholders.

In essence, directors owe a *personal* duty of care to their company, not to the individual members. In Percival v Wright (1902) the directors purchased shares from the plaintiffs while secretly negotiating to sell the company at a more favourable price. The court declined to upset the contract remarking that premature disclosure of the negotiations 'might well be against the best interests of the company'.

However, the directors may in particular circumstances owe duties to individual shareholders: for example, when they undertake to act as the shareholders' agents (Allen v Hyatt (1914)).

Directors have a duty to take into account the interests of employees as well as the interests of members. The statutory duty is owed to and enforceable by the company, not by the employees directly, so acts benefiting employees must also further the interests of the company. This provision does not change the directors' duties in a going concern, since benefits for the workforce have been held to be in the interests of the company (Hutton v West Cork Railway Co (1883)).

D & O insurance

A Directors' and Officers' liability policy will pay the costs of defending any UK director or officer from claims being brought against them and it is this defence element, coupled with the damages indemnity limit, which is of critical importance. Policies vary from one insurer to another (at the last count there are at least ten offering policies in the UK).

However, a specialist broker will be able to assist in the purchase of one of the most important insurance contracts available. It is essential to ensure that the insurer specifically states that he will pay defence costs *as they are incurred* and not wait until the outcome of any given trial. Nowadays legal processes can span three to five years and clearly one would not wish the policy to pay only on the verdict.

A number of D & O liability insurers ask for a list of the names of the directors and the officers to be insured. For obvious reasons this is sometimes difficult and time consuming particularly for large and complex companies and it is again important to have a policy that will cover all the directors and officers, whoever they are, to cater for any eventuality.

Particular issues arise with outside board insurance. It is possible when sitting on the board of a third party investee company to be held personally liable, albeit while carrying out the duties for the principal employer. D & O liability policies can be extended to include outside board directorships, but again this needs to be worked out carefully with a specialist broker.

Loss prevention

Although the risks and potential personal liabilities which directors face are serious, there are ways to guard against such risks: by observing proper standards of conduct, by acting with care, honesty and diligence and by ensuring that appropriate management systems are in place and are used. In the selection of directors it is important that a good balance is struck between the various needs of the company and factors such as the strength and skills of different directors. Board selection based purely on the old boy network is increasingly dangerous. Directors should bear in mind the following potential attributes:

- Objectivity.
- Inquisitiveness.
- Independence of mind.
- The ability to listen.
- Initiative.
- Imagination and original thinking.
- Communication skills.
- Coordination skills.
- Integrity.

If the composition of the board is properly balanced, with individuals working well together, and each director fulfils his responsibilities in a professional manner, the potential for individual directors to incur liabilities should be small. Every company and every individual is different and the appropriate composition of a board will vary considerably from one situation to another. The size and complexity of a company's business will largely dictate the number of directors which there should be on a board. It is, however, essential that all areas of the company's business activities are properly represented.

Re-evaluation of directors in terms of their track record and contribution must be part of any company's procedure. When new directors join the company it is incumbent on them to look at all aspects of the company, including its published accounts going back over the last few years, the minute book, subsidiary companies' report and accounts, and recent management accounts.

Additionally, new directors should probably meet the

company's professional advisers, get to know them and the background of the company. They should visit any of the company's operating premises and take a very close look at the financial position of the company with regard to bank facilities, cashflow and other obvious flash point areas. It would also be worth ensuring a D & O liability policy is in force.

When a Board is making a decision it is important that adequate information is available and that meetings are conducted in the manner prescribed by the company's Articles and recorded at all times with the documents being clear and correctly stored.

Claims and conclusion

It is often asked whether any claims have been made against directors and officers. Regrettably the answer is increasingly 'yes'. Awards totalling nearly £1m have been made against directors over the last 12 months. This does not take into account the legal costs incurred or the increasing number of cases that go unreported.

Policies are available which incorporate both professional indemnity and directors' and officers' liability into one contract, so both the company balance sheet and the director's personal liability can be catered for in one overall protection.

Policies for outside board cover only, shadow directorship cover only or for directors who do not require company reimbursement and indeed many other variations are also available depending on particular requirements.

Legislation and the cobweb of liability now surrounding directors and officers require a thorough understanding. The more this area is studied the more complex the issues become and therefore the more important it is to maintain adequate insurance to cover an unlimited personal liability.

In a limited liability company only the shareholders' liability is limited, not that of the directors.

9

External relations

Apart from a non-executive chairman, the independent directors are the only people around the board table who can genuinely look at their company from the outside in. They should use their position tactfully. The chairman and executives who think they are performing well are likely to feel uncomfortable, if not resentful, if blind spots are revealed by their independent colleagues.

The outside perspective is not only needed to monitor the work of the chairman and executives. A company is dynamic. It is likely to suffer pressures and face new opportunities from changes in the market place, from competitive products, new technology, trade tariffs and the like. One objective of board strategy is to anticipate at least some of these changes and to establish appropriate positions in advance with important groups such as shareholders, customers, suppliers, employees, and within the local community.

Economic performance inevitably has a heavy influence on external relationships and how smoothly they run. When a company is known to be in trouble, many problems occur. If a listed company, the share price will have fallen – shareholders having either sold, decided to seek a potential bidder or are clamouring for changes. There will also be trading complications;

customers may be seeking alternative suppliers which they regard as secure, and they may become slow payers. Suppliers will be demanding swift settlement.

As it is not possible to disguise the truth from employees, morale will deteriorate and the best people will be starting to leave. If profits start to recover from a remedial programme the board should take the opportunity to communicate with those connected with the business.

An external policy should be formulated by the board as a whole, but implemented by the chairman and executives. Independent directors should not normally be involved unless asked to participate in a particular programme. Their level of involvement can change dramatically if things go wrong – then they can be catapulted into the limelight to deal with a scandal or a fraud. Normally though, independent directors will be concerned with encouraging and monitoring their executive colleagues to work through creating the external profile of the business which will take many different forms. Six of these are considered in this chapter:

1 Projecting company strategy.
2 Speaking to shareholders.
3 Listening to shareholders.
4 Working with bankers.
5 Communicating with staff and outside parties.
6 An independent director's contribution.

1 Projecting company strategy

Public relations (PR) has an essential supportive role in implementing board strategy. If the board decides on a programme of acquisitions, opening new markets, diversification or rationalization, PR should be used to prepare the ground for future operations. For example, this might include targeting different audiences such as the media, institutions, other investors, employees, community groups and the like. Whatever a company's plans, there is almost always a need to influence external opinion. These are some instances of preparing the ground:

- An example of good PR strategy was employed by Nestlé in their bid for Rowntree. The bidder took great care to make their case to the people of York in general and with employees in particular.
- Conversely, if there is a downside risk of the company being acquired, there is a considerable advantage in mobilizing local feeling against the bid. This strategy was successfully used by Pilkington when fighting off an unwelcome bid from BTR. Another successful PR defensive strategy was waged by Higgs and Hill.
- A company may be planning to reduce costs by making individuals or groups work independently, as tried by Rank Xerox. A sensible strategy would be to test the idea with several sets of people to see how the plan affected their lives. If successful the programme should be reported in the house journal and in the local press before expanding the idea to other groups.
- A board may decide to close an obsolete plant where many of those made redundant will find it difficult to find other employment. The company demonstrates that it is willing to help those laid off with retraining, introductions to other employers, counselling or transfers to other parts of the company.

2 Speaking to shareholders

The chairman is the bridge between the board and the shareholders. Whatever message has been agreed by the board is then transmitted by the chairman, or perhaps delegated to the chief executive or finance director. There are three main reports in the life of a PLC that are handled by the board (some large companies report quarterly); these are the interim statements, preliminary settlements, and the annual report and accounts. The last forms the substance for the annual general meeting (AGM).

The practice of non-listed companies varies considerably. Some which have a number of outside shareholders may report in the same way as a PLC, others which are family controlled or venture capital investments, will content themselves with some form of AGM. Each board should seek its own practice based upon the needs of the shareholders and the resources of the board. How a medium sized PLC might deal with its reporting seasons is detailed below.

The report and accounts

A good set of accounts can make an average company look tolerable and a good business look excellent, which is why a wise board will give the matter both time and trouble. The report and accounts is primarily a statutory document for shareholders but it can also serve as an informing and selling document to customers, employees, trading partners, new shareholders etc. These are some of the considerations raised by Sir Adrian Cadbury in his book *The Company Chairman* (see References):

- Institutional shareholders typically own around 70% of most listed companies; they are generally long-term stockholders and are primarily interested in the board meeting their strategic targets. Since the beginning of the 1990s' recession, the institutions have become very interested in retaining the value of their investment.
- Private shareholders are by far the most numerous but, in a listed company, are unlikely to own more than 30% of the equity. Their objectives are legion. For example, some will have retained an interest in a previously acquired company, others may be interested in the product, a further group may have local associations. Some private shareholders have become much more adept than the professionals in spotting take-over candidates or companies with above average potential.
- New shareholders may be attracted to the company because they like the style of the business, believe it has good growth prospects, admire the management etc.
- Trading partners are important users of company information. For example, creditors will check for ability to pay and customers for continuity of supply. Other groups such as joint venture partners, licensors or potential principals will all be seeking assurances that the company is financially and commercially robust.

When compiling the report and accounts Sir Adrian Cadbury suggests the following guidelines:

- The report and accounts is a permanent record of the company's performance for the year. It will become part of stockbrokers' files, investors' libraries, credit analysts' references and find a place in business libraries.
- Although many people will have an input to the document, one pen should be discernible from each part such as the chairman's statement, chief executive's report etc.
- The chairman's statement should review the company as a whole, report progress and describe any remedial action taken to bring the company back on track.
- The executive report will normally cover the work of the individual trading subsidiaries and progress against a declared strategy.
- Some companies combine the executive statement with a report to the employees enclosed in the report and accounts.
- Institutions are now requiring more details of the directors, a brief curriculum vitae and the composition of board groups such as the chairman's or audit committees. The International Stock Exchange is also requiring details of directors' share transactions during the year as well as the holdings at the year-end.

Apart from publishing and distributing the report and accounts, listed companies will have to communicate with their shareholders on three separate occasions.

Interim statement

After 6 months of the financial year it is normal for a listed company to issue an unaudited interim statement. This will cover the first half of the trading year and there is generally a commentary on current activity and how it might impact on the end-of-year result.

Most companies' interim figures are not noted with any particular interest unless there have been changes in the company, perhaps following an acquisition. Another focus of interest might be the trading conditions for a particular industry. Once the statement has been agreed by the board, it is usual for it to be checked by the stockbroker and public relations adviser (if any) before release. The statement will often include a telephone number where the chairman or chief executive can be contacted to answer any questions.

Preliminary statement

This is an important statement used by analysts and commentators who are more concerned with share price performance than viewing the company as a whole. The report will be audited and show a comparison with the previous year plus a written view on the year's trading. Some boards may also wish to show a summary of the balance sheet if there has been concern of any weakness, perhaps through over indebtedness.

Cadbury and others recommend that the chairman, and perhaps other members of the board should make themselves available to financial analysts and the financial press (in that order) after the preliminary results are announced.

Annual general meeting

This is a formal occasion when shareholders vote on the statutory agenda; this should include accepting the accounts, appointing directors, auditors etc. The meeting is taken by the chairman and Cadbury recommends that detailed preparations be made to anticipate questions of procedure, shareholders' queries, intrusions by pressure groups etc. He also recommends that all questions are taken by the chairman himself with specific points being covered by individual directors after the meeting.

The AGM is considered by some boards to be an occasion for meeting and entertaining shareholders. One enterprising company organized the lunch seating plan to include middle managers, staff and operatives acting as hosts. Shareholders were delighted to have the opportunities of meeting others apart from board members.

The chairman and executive directors should also make themselves available to financial analysts and the press whether the offer is accepted or not. One important occasion is after the release of the preliminary results. Others can be board presentations to analysts, fund managers and potential shareholders either on company visits or at the stockbroker's offices. It is also becoming the custom for individual analysts to make informal company visits when they hope to gain a deeper insight to both the company and its managers.

3 Listening to shareholders

Most institutions take an interest in their investments and in turn like to communicate their own ideas to company boards. This two-way traffic is extremely important but may be severely distorted when fund managers are adjudicating the relative merits of take-over bids. Whatever the institutional workload, PR advisers are likely to recommend that chairmen and senior executives make themselves available to major shareholders at particular times in the financial calendar.

Institutional liaison is nearly always the duty of the chairman and chief executive; the independent directors are there to ensure that the board keeps open good channels of communication with shareholders as a whole and specifically with the major institutions. Independent directors may find themselves asked about their company through informal City or other contacts but they would be unwise to see themselves as a spokesman.

From time to time, the institutions issue guidelines to listed companies that should be heeded by wise boards. One of the most recent is the document issued by the Institutional Shareholders Committee (ISC) during April 1991 which sets out a statement of 'Best Practice on the Role and Duties of Directors'. As the institutions own over 70% of all listed companies, boards should listen closely to their owners' recommendations.

The potential power of the institutions is immense and if for some reason a board feels at odds with some of the ISC's ideas, the company's case should be put to the ISC's Investment Committee to seek an agreed solution; it is preferable to take this course rather than risk a public rebuttal. These are the most important issues raised by the paper:

- The roles of chairman and chief executive should be separate because there have been instances of excessive power concentration damaging performance, or even worse. If the board decides that one person should occupy the two positions then the institutions would like to see a committee made up of independent directors periodically reviewing the position.

- A compensation committee of independent directors should be appointed to agree the executive compensation package including remuneration, profit sharing, service contracts and the award of options. This is similar to the Chairman's committee (see Chapter 8), and its members should be recorded in the report and accounts.
- The company Articles should include a maximum, as well as a minimum number of directors without necessarily stipulating the balance between executive and outside board members.
- Shareholders would like to see complete independence for the outside directors which means that they should not be retired senior executives or professional advisers; they should also not hold directorships in the same industry without disclosure to the board.
- The institutions would like an audit committee appointed comprised mainly of independent directors. They also recommend an ad hoc group be formed to monitor an arrangement such as a buy-out of a significant asset involving a board member.

4 Working with bankers

It is always prudent to keep bankers in touch with the board's thinking. If there is to be bad news, no sensible board will allow their bankers to hear this through a third party. Contact at senior level is essential; some boards make a point of entertaining their bank managers at some evening of the year, usually after the AGM, which helps a harmonious relationship.

Banking contact is usually made through the executive directors. Apart from day-to-day business, it is sensible to make formal banking contact at the time of the interim and preliminary statements before the results are made public. It might be a good idea to use the meeting to report current year progress and if any action is needed to bring the company back to its stated strategy.

Liaison with bankers is even more important if things go seriously wrong and the company finds itself in the hands of the bank's intensive care unit. Not surprisingly, many managements can become very defensive when their policies are in tatters and it is up to the independent directors to advise caution.

Intensive care units are very realistic about their work which can be made much easier if a board understands what they have to do. Independent directors can help by anticipating their procedures:

- Before ever meeting the intensive care unit, the directors should institute a strict regime of cash control, cost reduction, surplus asset disposal and debt collection. This is likely to generate pleasant surprise, and the tough action may even result in softer instructions to the investigating accountants who will almost invariably be appointed.
- It may be galling to have investigating accountants asking awkward questions about procedures and policies but acceptance is sensible and will reduce the cost to the company, not to the bank. The company is wise to prepare documents and files for easy checking. The investigators will also be required to give an assessment of executive and board competence.
- The crisis remedy is almost certainly to include reducing costs and unwinding debt by selling surplus assets. These actions are seldom palatable but it is preferable for the company to take the remedial measures on its own terms, rather than have other ideas imposed (see Chapter 3). If the programme is acceptable to the intensive care unit then the company will be in a stronger position to negotiate on other demands such as a change of directors.

5 The company, its employees and the local community

Many boards make a practice of preparing a separate report to employees, some of whom may be shareholders. This is an important document and some companies arrange to hold employee AGMs to explain board policy and how it will affect the working of the company.

Companies contribute to their local community depending upon their maturity, inclination and size. For example, it would be unrealistic for a start-up operation or a management buy-out struggling to pay off debts to devote the same time to local affairs as a large mature group. Non-executive directors living near a company could be in a good position to suggest what could be done and when.

Most companies have far more demand upon their generosity than their resources can meet so it is useful to know a yardstick developed by United Biscuits and described by Cadbury in *The Company Chairman* (see References). Sir Adrian defines a company as being licensed by society to produce the goods and services that it needs and he cites approvingly United Biscuits' Per Cent Club whereby 0.5% of pre-tax profits are spent on community projects in Britain. This in no way implies that Cadbury Schweppes or United Biscuits are 'soft touches' but it does mean that the group has a set of objectives that are pursued alongside its commercial interests. These are how some of them work:

Wealth creation: The company takes an active part in sponsoring education, particularly in partnership with local schools. The company tries to find appropriate work experience for pupils and teachers, provides teaching material and equipment, funds school enterprise schemes and sponsors students.

Enterprise: The group is an active member of Business in the Community which sponsors new enterprises being set up in Britain's older industrial areas. It was felt that it was better to channel the work in conjunction with other companies than to operate alone.

Community clubs: Cadbury Schweppes works with local organizations which have employee associations depending on their needs. Clubs and associations are seldom particularly well managed but the company consults the committees how best they can be helped. This may mean either seconding management skills or providing cash support. Employees are also encouraged to take an active role.

6 An independent director's contribution

In the normal course of events, independent directors are not involved with their company's customers or suppliers unless they have direct contacts. Most independent directors will be happy to arrange introductions with people they know but would be unwise to become involved in negotiations unless the executives specifically ask for their help. Independent directors should strongly encourage senior executives and even the chairman to spend as much time as possible learning about their most important customers.

Many independent directors make a point of learning about their company's business 'countenance' by visiting trade fairs and exhibitions; they regard this as an excellent way of meeting the sales people and assessing competitors. It provides an opportunity to walk around other stands, meet competitors and watch how the salespeople conduct themselves around the stand. Peter Benton suggests that much can be learned by independent directors actually spending a day with the representatives (see Chapter 14).

Some executives make use of independent directors to test the efficiency of the sales organization by making telephone enquiries and observing how individuals respond to requests for information or prices. How far an independent director can go in testing the system depends very much upon the culture of the company and the rivalries around the board table. It is quite legitimate to visit exhibitions but testing the system may be regarded as spying.

10

An independent director's contribution to strategy

To a seventeenth-century general, having a stratagem meant working out a trick or ruse to outwit a foe. The word changed to strategy in the early part of the nineteenth century when describing the work put in by a military commander like Wellington when planning the Peninsula campaign.

Now the military staff colleges teach strategy as the long-term planning and execution of a campaign and tactics to describe shorter-term action or manoeuvres. In the introduction to Professor Brian Houlden's book *Understanding Company Strategy* (see References), Sir Adrian Cadbury has neatly described strategy as the need for a business to 'deliver a decisive advantage over what our competitors may have in mind'. The Duke would almost certainly have approved.

Ultimately, strategy is almost always about choosing which product/market areas the company is going to address, and the broad routes that will be used to penetrate them. Despite this common thrust, in practice the word is used to describe widely varied aspects of company aspiration or posture:

• TI's total shift from its steel tubing related activities of the 1960s to its present focus on selected niches, each capable of sustainable technological and world market share leadership.

- ICI's Paints division, which has developed a major world market share in its chosen sector.
- BAe's moves in the 1980s to add property and automotive activities to its defence business, in order to smooth cyclic effects, and make property gains.
- Amstrad's moves into and out of audio and computer sectors.
- Hanson's corporate dealing aimed at seeking maximization of shareholder values.

In the case of small to medium companies, independent directors often find it difficult to persuade their busy executive colleagues to give much time to thinking about the future. In this setting, 'strategy' may be viewed as no more than budgeting; all that needs to be done is to make some assumptions about sales volumes and costs then turn the whole matter over to the financial staff.

After some pressure from the independent directors, such executives may produce a 'strategic plan', perhaps to move a distribution point nearer to the market. A more dangerous response is for the executives to read a book or attend a course which urges a strategy of growth through acquisitions that will 'improve earnings per share at 20% compound for the next five years!' It is, after all, more appealing to travel the world buying companies rather than chip away to improve the performance of existing businesses! The independent director's role can be critical.

It is generally argued that, in larger companies, the chairman should have prime responsibility for strategic thinking, while leaving the executives to provide the staff work and manage the business. This view implies an important supporting role for the independent directors. Like other board members, they have a responsibility for the long-term continuity of the company; but being more detached, they are often better placed than the executives to perceive opportunities and recognize downside risks.

No winning strategy can be successful unless the 'core' business is well founded which means that the existing businesses should be profitable and run by competent people. Pursuing an expansionist strategy from a weak base, particularly through acquisitions, has been the epitaph of many companies. It is said that the main insolvency practitioners have a list of individuals who have consistently followed this approach and left a trail of wrecked companies behind them – all the professionals have to do is to wait!

Those wishing to learn about the theory and practice of strategy should read from the extensive literature on the subject (see References). In no way is this chapter a substitute. It does, however, comment on four main areas where the independent director is most likely to be able to contribute.

1 Relevant prior experience

Frequently, independent directors have seen situations at first hand, where there is a resemblance to the current status of the company.

On occasion, this will be where the industry or market is familiar to the independent director, so that he can deploy his knowledge of it in the board's work on developing strategy. Examples could be prior experience of dealing with a major supplier, or of the political posture of a foreign government.

In other cases, the experience will not relate to the same industry or market, but to other aspects of developing strategy. Examples of this would be a major redesign of the organization structure, or flotation and the particular problems this entails.

To the extent that the executives have similar experience to that of the independent directors, little may be added; but where the independent directors have experiences in different fields, companies, markets and circumstances, they can make a key input to the strategic development.

2 'It feels wrong'

As an individual's experience accrues, sensitivity increases about the likelihood that a given assertion or forecast is true. The result is known by many names, for example, feel, nose, business judgement, nous, being streetwise. It develops as a result of combining experience of the world with an individual naturally receptive to this type of learning experience.

When senior businessmen are asked which qualities are

particularly valuable in the independent director, this quality, 'feel' figures high in the list.

3 Specialized knowledge

Expert knowledge can be of great value to a company's strategic planning. Often this will apply in advanced technology situations, or areas such as international politics. Other areas can also be of major importance, but more in tactical than strategic issues; an example here would be legal expertise.

4 'Can see it coming'

One further area where executive directors are often on relatively unfamiliar ground, concerns business cycles. Often independent directors are older than the executives, and are more conscious of having lived through several oscillations, and therefore tend to see the cycles as a natural part of the backdrop against which business is conducted. The consequences for strategic plans can be significant. As this area may be less familiar, it is expanded at greater length below.

No board strategy should be complete without building in assumptions of regular periods of boom or slump such as have occurred regularly in the post-war period, but have in fact been a feature of business life for at least 200 years (see References).

The most obvious cycle was that identified by Clement Juglar in the 1860s when he reported that booms and busts move in a series of regular waves with a duration of seven to 11 years. Juglar based his work on interest rate fluctuations and raw material prices in Britain, France and the USA and divided his cycle into four phases (Figure 10.1).

These are the phases in more detail.

Prosperity

A typical prosperity phase occurred when the western world

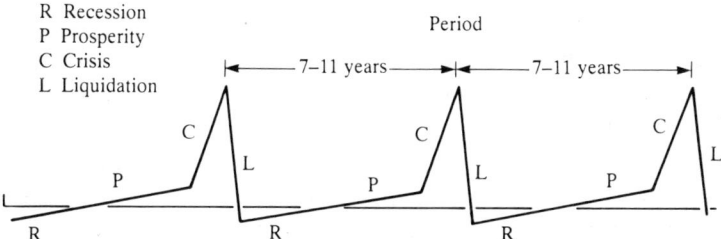

Figure 10.1 *Idealized Juglar cycle*

moved out of recession in 1983. It was the time that risks could be taken with expansion plans and borrowings increased in the anticipation that the boom would last for at least five years. The beginning of this phase is marked by low raw material prices and interest rates – a good time strategically to negotiate long-term supply and borrowing contracts.

Financial crisis

At some point the economy becomes overheated and interest rates start to rise with increasing debt levels accompanied usually by higher material prices. Wise managements will have made a study of the cycles and put together a contingency plan towards the end of the previous phase to reduce costs and unwind surplus assets. This is essential to protect against being squeezed between lower margins and higher costs as the crisis develops.

Liquidation

The debt mountain now starts to unwind because all debts have to be settled at some time. One of three things can happen: the first is that the debt is paid. The second is that the debt is repudiated by the debtor becoming insolvent. The third is a compromise where some agreement is reached between the parties. During this phase there is a scramble for cash while assets are liquidated in an effort to reduce debts.

Recession

It takes some time for banks and traders to regain confidence allowing credit to be used in transactions after its collapse during the previous phase. Recessions last for varying periods depending upon debt levels. For example, in 1991 the US debt to Gross National Product ratio was at similar levels to those in 1931. This would imply a recession lasting for several years.

In practice, many economists judge the length of cycles from one 'spike' of interest rates to the next as shown in Figure 10.2. This is the movement of the US 90-day Treasury Bill Yield from 1920 to 1991 which peaked every nine to 11 years (apart from the war years). The last spike was in 1981 so it is reasonable to expect a peak in 1992/3.

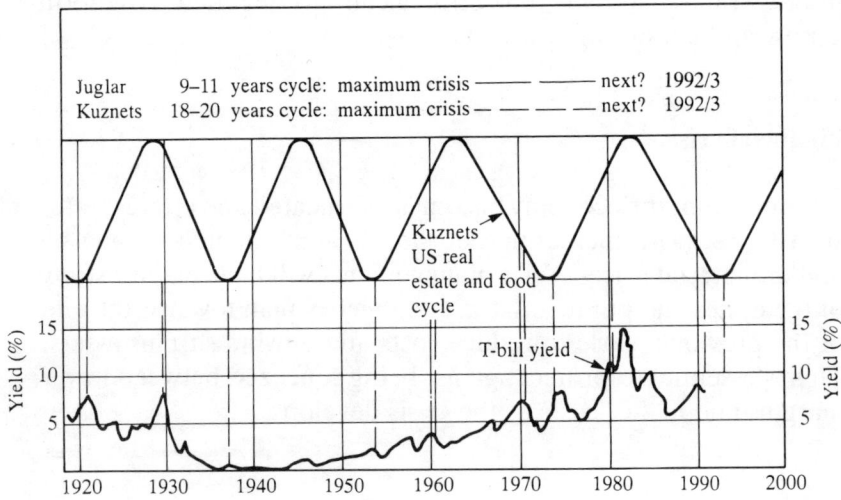

Figure 10.2 *Juglar and Kuznets cycles 1920–1995*

The chart also shows another cycle called the Kuznets or US Real Estate Cycle. The pattern of US real estate prices was established by Simon Kuznets, an American economist, during the 1930s who identified a cycle of price rises and falls over a 18–20 year period. The low points are set out every 18.6 years in the chart because the Kuznets coincides (whether by chance or due to some logical linkage) with a climatic period of the same duration – every time the cycle has bottomed it has become very dry in the upper latitudes of the northern hemisphere resulting in high commodity prices. The next low point is in 1992/3.

An example

The following example illustrates how independent directors contributed to the work of the board of an engineering group based in the Mid West of the USA. The light engineering division had not been performing well, and one of the independent directors drew attention to the fact that by 1979 the economy was coming to the end of a nine to 11 year cycle, with the likelihood that interest rates would soon start to rise.

The board decided that a survey should be made, and set up a group for the purpose including an independent director having experience of appraising businesses. The stages in the evaluation process appear below.

There were five businesses all of which had some connection with automotive, commercial vehicle or mechanical handling; the customer either fitted the component(s) into an assembly (original equipment or OE), or sold them directly or through distributors. There are five steps in the assessment followed in the study, only two of which are set out in detail.

Step 1

The financial performance of each company over at least three years was listed. The balance sheet was reported as well as the operating statement.

Step 2

The main accounts representing 80–85% of sales were listed by name and category. A table was drawn up showing the allocation of each company's sales by market segment.

Step 3

Table 10.1 lists the five companies (called A to E) as at 31 March 1987. A makes servicing equipment for customers in mechanical engineering, commercial vehicles, and the military, selling directly or through distributors. Sales for the year were $23m, pre-tax profits were $1.8m and assets employed were $12m. The other companies were analysed in a similar way.

Table 10.1 *The five companies as at 31 March 1987*

Main products	Customer categories	Sales ($m)	PBT ($m)	Assets ($m)
A Servicing equipment	Mechanical, commercial vehicles distributors	23	1.8	12.0
B Hydraulic, lube and pneumatic components	Automative, commercial vehicle OE	12	0.9	8.0
C Hydraulic and lube systems	CV and machine tool OE	13	1.1	12.0
D Hydraulic and automotive and pneumatic hoses	OE, mechanical handling and smaller a/cs	20	2.3	9.0
E Hydraulic, air and oil filters	Automotive, CV OE and smaller accounts	18	0.2	9.0

Note: Overlaps were apparent between divisions B and C, D and E, and there was a possible case for concentration if the combined management were strong enough, and costs and/or sales could be improved.

Step 4: Scoring relative strengths

The strengths and weaknesses of the key managers in each division were assessed to devise the best combination in case concentration should emerge as a serious option. The divisions were clearly production driven so it was decided to rate management strength in marketing, production, general management and financial control on a scale of 1–10.

Marketing was a composite divided into three: these were distribution, original equipment sales and the capacity to innovate. This is what was included under the three headings:

Distributor marketing required encouraging dealers to stock and sell the company's products against competing lines. The best product (for the dealers) was nationally known, was supported by advertising and had large margins. In short, profits were easy.

Proficient marketing to distributors required the sales force to establish a close relationship with the distributor and to provide help with field selling. The dealers were mainly in the following trades: engineering, automotive, mechanical handling, earth moving, general engineers, and commercial vehicles.

Original equipment accounts were defined as those where components were built into a final product such as a car, commercial vehicle, machine tool, fork-lift truck, or excavator. The selling tended to be working with engineers but keeping closely in touch with buyers and quality control people.

Innovation was defined as the division's ability to modify, adapt, repackage and find new markets in the given market sectors. For example, a company selling hydraulic hoses to a fork-lift truck manufacturer might adapt the fittings so they could be assembled on site with a new hose to save break-down time.

Assessments were also made under three other headings:

Production: the ability to manage the plant, administratively and technically.

General management ability.

Financial control over costs and working capital.

Each division was assessed under these headings on a scale of 1–10; these were the ratings:

Rating
10 Exceptional professional ability and performance.
8–9 Very good performance using imagination and initiative.
6–7 Good general ability with a thoughtful energetic approach.
5   Average competence
3–4 Fair ability, operates by rote, nothing new is learned.
1–2 Low competence level.

Table 10.2 *The five companies' ratings*

	Sales/ Assets	PBT/ Sales	PBT/ Assets	Market-ing	Produc-tion	General manage-ment	Financial control	Total	Poss %
A	1.9	7.8	14.8	21	3	4	4	32	53
B	1.5	7.5	11.3	14	7	3	5	29	41
C	1.1	8.4	9.2	28	4	3	3	38	54
D	2.2	11.5	25.3	23	6	7	7	43	61
E	2.0	1.1	2.2	16	3	5	3	27	39

The companies in the division were now rated according to the specializations described above with a financial assessment (Table 10.2).

For example Company A had a rating asset turnover to sales of 1.9, a return on sales of 7.8% and a return on assets of 14.8%. The company's marketing was rated 21, production 3, general management 4 and financial control 4. The total was 32 and ranked 53 out of a possible 100.

Step 5: Assessing the results

Clearly the top performer is D with a return of capital of 25.3% and a performance rating of 61%. The general manager is very able with a good potential for managing a larger unit or combining with another company, possibly E.

Company A is the only company in the division producing equipment and the low rating for production, general management and financial control suggests that the team needs more backing. The great strength of the business is marketing so it is worth attacking the weak links.

Company C shows a high return on sales but low assets turnround – too much capital is needed to generate sales. The company does not score well on production, general management or financial control suggesting that it might be sensible to look into the make/buy policy.

Companies B and E are the low performers being 20% below the leaders; they are clearly candidates for either disposal or amalgamation.

Short–medium term plan

This is how the short to medium term (2–3 years) strategic plan was implemented.

Companies B and C, D and E were amalgamated under the most competent general managers. This resulted in considerable savings of cost from lower administrative overheads and margin improvement from dropping unprofitable lines. Margins were further improved by opening up new accounts and increasing product added value.

In Company A, specialist in servicing equipment, the team found some opportunities for modifying the product range.

Electronic sensors and other instruments improved the performance of the electromechanical products, and other new products were brought forward. Modified products were also offered in extended markets. Standardized lubrication equipment was mounted on mobile trailers or vehicles which reduced the down-time and maintenance and repairs for costly excavators and other mobile plant. The same thinking was applied to servicing for armoured and other military field vehicles.

The other part of the strategy was not successful. The managers decided to expand into the European Community by making an acquisition of a company with similar products to A in France. The analysis showed good product cross-fertilization, the markets were similar and A's management was enthusiastic. The prospect was confirmed by a visit by the vice-president of finance who spoke fluent French.

The acquisition failed for four reasons:

1 Differing engineering standards required considerable product modification before there was any export/import interchange.
2 The acquiring management found that the actual inventory values produced much lower margins than had been forecast in the budget at time of purchase. It was hoped that the problem could be solved by higher prices but by then the economic cycle was ending and the company was plunged rapidly into loss.
3 Under the terms of the contract, the previous owners were allowed to retire and new professional management was brought in from outside the business. Unfortunately the negotiating team had neglected to include any performance criteria in the consideration so that many sales contacts and much business 'nous' disappeared with the vendors. In an attempt to salvage the situation, the general manager from the parent company had to be seconded for long periods of time to manage the business.
4 The negotiating team had failed to find out that firing people in France was much more difficult and expensive than in the USA. Bringing costs into line with the market meant lengthy and expensive haggling with the local union and prefecture officials who were determined to wring every possible concession from the inexperienced management team.

11

If things go wrong

There is no such thing as 'bad luck' in business only bad management. If any executive states that the company is going through a rough time due to events outside his control – and he is not trying to do anything about it – he should not be believed. There will always be a real problem to be unearthed. If the company is put in the hands of administrators, all directors will be held as responsible as the executive directors if the business is deemed to have traded wrongfully while insolvent.

So, what can an outside director do to help? If things have gone wrong, the executive directors should admit their mistake and propose remedies. The board can then rally round and collectively help to put things right. Matters are quite different if the error has either been disregarded or concealed in some way through 'creative accounting', then the board has to go to action stations. This chapter covers these eventualities in five parts:

1 What can go wrong.
2 What the executives should recommend.
3 Finding out the hard way.

4 Asking the right questions.
5 Into action.

1 What can go wrong

Companies get into trouble either because they have made an unwise decision and not put it right, or they have neglected fundamental principles of survival. These are some of the most common failings which should alert wary individuals. They are divided into four main categories.

Miscalculating the business cycle

The boom phase of the business cycle is turning negative. After a wonderful run of expansion when demand exceeds supply, inflationary pressures cause governments to increase interest rates which steer the economy towards a recession. Business is poor, costs are rising and there is an acknowledgement that stringent action needs to be taken to reduce costs and fund debt. Outside directors should be aware of the approach of these forces and report them to the board.

Acquisitions fail to come up to expectations

An acquisition has gone seriously wrong. Many companies went into mergers, for what seemed excellent reasons at the time, but a number of these have gone terribly sour – often for the same reasons:

- The acquired company was in a financial mess and the profits at the time of acquisition were illusory. In most cases deals failed either due to executive incompetence, over-optimistic assumptions or lack of synergy. When things go wrong, it is rare that the same managers who made the mistake are the ones to repair the damage.
- The acquiring company did not realize the contribution of individuals who left the acquired company shortly after

completion. Customers either transferred loyalty elsewhere or followed the retiring executives when they re-started on their own.

- The acquiring company made a series of incorrect decisions leading to the departure of some of the target company's best and most experienced people.
- The timing of the acquisition occurred at the end of the business cycle boom phase when activity levels were declining and interest rates rising. This is particularly important when the acquisition is made on borrowed money.
- The acquired company had some hidden liability such as a major loss-making contract that was absorbing excessive resources. The problem is made worse if the parent company was forced to give a performance bond or bank guarantees at the time of the acquisition.

Overtrading

The company is overtrading, implying that it is attempting to expand from too small a financial base and cannot raise additional working capital.

- One example is the 'flywheel' effect where a company needs to acquire or generate additional income to pay the rising interest charges. The technique can work well at the beginning of a business cycle. It is a disaster towards the end.
- A period of declining margins resulting in a series of losses has wrung the working capital value down to an unworkable level.

Unrealistic business judgement

- The company has taken on a contract that is absorbing excessive management and financial resources which will seriously hurt the business if nothing is done.
- An expected event such as a potentially profitable contract or a new product fails to materialize.
- The cost assumptions used for pricing are flawed and contracts have been taken at a loss. The fault is particularly dangerous at the start of a business cycle – possibly accompanied by overtrading – or during a time of inflation.

- A major customer switches from a product or technology leaving a quantity of unsaleable inventory or unused plant. This can also occur when a company is too reliant on one customer.
- A start-up company that never achieves its forecast sales. This could be the case of a business where the results never reached the original assumptions or a small contractor that did not learn the secret of winning the next contract while completing the last.
- The leveraged buy-out that just never squeezed cash out of the business to pay off enough debt.

2 What the executives should do

It is always better for executives to take the right corrective decisions without being prodded by the independent directors. They are running the company and are in the best possible position to know the threat to profitability or the balance sheet.

The executive directors should now propose measures to reduce costs and fund debt. These are some of the key issues:

- They should make a detailed operational review of all activities that are, or might become, marginal. The analysis should include the true profitability of each product or service with the associated assets.
- Turning surplus assets into cash quickly is more important than receiving the best price. The executives may show their skill by adapting parts of obsolete products and selling these in markets that do not compete with their regular lines.
- Steps should be taken to protect cash through hedging vulnerable currencies, protecting deposits (by moving out of risky banks) and improving availability.
- Customers are more reluctant to pay for goods and services when doubtful whether they will receive future supplies. Creditors should be assured that paying their bills will buy working capital, not be sucked up by the secured creditors.
- Inventory will be prone to obsolescence. It would be good to hear the executives reviewing proposals for Just In Time or other techniques for reducing inventory size.
- Stock market values generally decline at the end of a business cycle. Strategic stock holdings should be carefully reviewed

because, if sold, they can probably be bought back more cheaply later.

- When large redundancy costs are involved it is much better to retain some skills by making individuals independent (Houston *Avoiding Adversity*, see References).
- Contracting out services will often save overheads and transfer fixed to variable costs.
- Costs can be saved by re-negotiating long-term liabilities such as property leases, purchase agreements and labour contracts.
- Costs may be converted from fixed to variable through judiciously unwinding groups of people and assets that could become independent.
- Product life cycles are likely to reduce which may require additional expenditure on development. This may also entail extra spending on market research.
- The business will not survive unless major customers can be persuaded to stay. Account responsibilities should be reviewed which may also entail an overhaul of customer service procedures. This may be checked by someone outside the company asking for a quotation to learn how well the system works.
- The balance sheet is the key to continuing solvency, realistic asset values should be assigned to all items of working capital and liabilities correctly stated.

3 Finding out the hard way

Most people find it difficult to admit their mistakes – aggressive executives find it almost impossible. Most go wrong because their management styles have not changed despite altered business conditions. Delaying action is fatal and any attempt to cover up errors puts outside directors in a very difficult position. They may complain that they have not been given the relevant data but, as board members, they still share an equal responsibility to the executives.

Ultimately the only real crisis facing a company is to run out of cash which means that accounts cannot be paid as they arise. With any luck, that condition should be some way down the line from preliminary warnings that may be spotted by independent directors:

- The company is slow in paying its bills signalled by an increase in creditor days. This will not be immediately evident unless there is a working capital statement or pro-forma balance sheet with the board papers. Independent directors can usually tell when there is a problem if the finance director is called urgently out from meetings by a slip of paper smuggled past the chairman. It is time to be concerned if he or she is away for some time and returns with a worried look.
- The chief executive announces several small redundancy measures – just to cut out the surplus fat! A clear minded chief executive will announce plans covering one or more departments or divisions based on an analysis that will have been first presented to the board. An indecisive chief executive will tackle the matter piecemeal, and then only when pushed.
- Business is tight, prices are lowered and too many small orders are accepted. The board papers will show reduced sales and probably declining margins. An outside director may not know how bad things really are unless there is evidence of trading down, increased numbers of credit notes and defecting customers.
- Good people are starting to leave. This is a very serious matter and can be a sign of declining morale and frustrated prospects; one clear sign is to watch for furtive groups of people in the offices or around the shop floor. They are worried too. The goods inward department is probably the first to hear of difficulties through delivery drivers.
- If the company is listed, the share price has fallen and the PE ratio is low for the sector. This may be due to stockbroker circulars, market rumours or leaks from competitors. There may also be talk that the company is an acquisition candidate.
- Board papers report continuing losses from certain divisions or subsidiaries. On questioning, the executives express future optimism but do nothing.
- The executives report that the banks would 'like to be brought up to date' on current trading. The company may be in difficulty if there are a number of banks and no clear leader with whom to negotiate.
- Secured creditors such as the banks appoint a firm of investigating accountants. This is a worrying sign that cannot be disguised however much it may be disparaged. Insolvency people (which is what they are) are hard realistic individuals who will look

behind the current trading assumptions and balance sheet values.

4 Asking the right questions

It is bad news for the executives if the independent directors learn the truth about the company's finances through questioning or observation. They must first determine the extent of the problem; second they have to deal with the management situation. Finally they have to decide the action to be taken and whom to tell.

If a company is short of cash, it can only mean one of the following:

- Trading losses have reduced the capacity to fund its working capital from debt collection, asset disposal or raising funds from external sources. It will seldom be possible for even the most 'creative' accountant to disguise losses – even if some are taken as extraordinary items.
- Receivables cannot be collected, either because they do not exist or they are so contested that they will not be paid in full.
- Inventory cannot be turned into cash at the balance sheet value either through obsolescence, quality defects or incorrect valuation.
- Cash balances are shown in the balance sheet but are unavailable for making payments because banks refuse to release the cash. One tell-tale sign may be the disposal of funds to obscure or unusual foreign banks.
- Creditors are understated either because there are off balance-sheet items, undisclosed contractual liabilities or potential law suits.

In these circumstances, outside directors should insist on the following:

- A cash flow statement and a pro-forma balance sheet at each meeting which will show any deterioration in the working capital position. The finance director might complain about the extra work but most of the data should be collected for a monthly trial balance in any case.

- A debtor ageing report. All credit controllers worth their salt should have the facts at their fingertips.
- A creditor ageing report which realistically sets out liabilities.

The status of receivables should be assessed:

- Each of the major outstanding debts should be listed and a case history produced on each.
- Some of the delays may be due to internal problems such as product quality, credit notes, incomplete contracts, financial problems etc.
- The executives most closely concerned with the debt should make regular progress reports and report on the action taken. It may be necessary to ask for agreed progress payments, perhaps backed by bills of exchange or more secure instruments.
- If the debtor is particularly large or important, the chairman or chief executive could visit the company and clear any outstanding queries.
- The procedure should question whether the debt collection routines are adequate. Is the credit control good enough, are the salesmen directly involved with debt collection, is supply withheld from late payers?
- It is a wise procedure for only the known good debtors to be used for working capital calculations. Reports on the large doubtful debts should be shown separately.
- Bad debts can also be caused by poor invoicing and specification, bad quality, incorrect quantities, sloppy credit note procedures etc.

The following action should be taken to check the inventory:

- Inventory valuation: if there are concerns, this seriously questions previous assumptions about profitability and casts doubts on the auditors' reliability.
- Stock items should turn over from weeks to months depending on the type of business, any longer period casts doubt on the book valuation. A list of items should be prepared in descending value and the annual turnover worked out. From this, the slow movers may be isolated.
- The list is likely to be dominated by some ageing or obsolescent

products. These should be segregated to find out the turnover of the remainder.

- Can slow moving or obsolescent products be sold at a discount in secondary markets to avoid a conflict with current sales to primary customers? Alternatively they may be assembled into other assemblies, sold for scrap or just dumped.
- Whatever the verdict, ensure that the remaining inventory items are correctly valued and the disposable items are reported separately.
- The board should be informed of any work in progress or contracts that may appear incorrectly valued in the accounts. Depending upon the accounting treatment, some unjustified profit may have been taken for part completed work. In a few cases, was shown as an asset has turned out to be a liability because the customer has issued a counter claim. These are serious matters.

The position of outstanding contracts should be checked:

- If there doubts about a contract's value or progress a report should be made on the stage valuations and whether these have been endorsed by the customer. This may be a complicated business involving site visits and customer meetings.
- If disputed contracts can be remedied and customer relations mended all well and good. If not, there may be real problems which could put future trading in doubt. Whatever happens, contractual problems occupy a great deal of time – first to understand the issues, next to consider the realities.

Damage limitation

- Murphy's Law states the only thing you can rely on are creditor valuations. However, do not take these as gospel – they may be understated through disputed claims or onerous contracts that are not included in their entirety. At this stage it is unwise to ask too many questions, just assess the downside risk.

5 Into action

The board should now know the worst. If the company is at risk of failure then the board should follow Route 1. If the position can be restored then Route 2 would be appropriate.

Route 1: The company is in danger of wrongful trading

Whoever takes charge around the board table must be exceptionally clearheaded and have good legal and accounting advice.

- Take immediate control of cash. This includes all incoming cheques, cheque books and items that are readily cashable.
- Ensure that no purchase orders over a certain level, say £1,000, are issued without permission.
- Stop recruitment and do not incur fresh liabilities without express permission. Scrutinize any agreed expenditure, such as foreign travel, and cancel everything that is not absolutely necessary.
- Offer inducement for early payments and come to terms with any disputed debts. Also turn any readily saleable surplus items or inventory into cash, see 4 above.
- Recast the cash flow statement. If there is a hope that the company can meet its debts as they arise (or as negotiated) then well and good. Put a really tough person in charge of the cash position, consult your solicitor on your intended action and tell the bank. If the secured creditors have not put in a reporting accountant they will certainly do so now. Cooperate fully with whoever is appointed.
- If the creditors cannot be paid, do not prevaricate. Advise the board that the company is in danger of trading while insolvent and, subject to legal opinion, advise the creditors immediately.

Route 2: Sorting out the mess

The independent directors have discovered the deteriorating position though questioning, implying that the executive directors were either ignorant or fraudulent. They have two basic choices:

- They can accept that the executives, supported by the chairman, had good grounds for believing that the company was not at risk. For example, it might be argued that a new contract was on the point of being signed or a new product launch would be successful.
- Sometimes last ditch efforts work, but mostly the directors should be highly sceptical. If the board accepts that a genuine mistake has been made, they may decide to allow the executives to continue, providing they adopt the agenda in 2 above.

If the board is divided:

- There could be a board minority who insist on immediate action but the majority refuses. In these circumstances, the minority should ensure that their proposal and its refusal, is minuted. They should then resign, reserving the right to inform the shareholders and banks of their action.
- There is a board majority for immediate action and the minority, which may include the chairman and executives disagree. The majority can then appoint a new chairman and chief executive, if needed, and take control. These are dangerous waters, full of legal problems should the minority now seek to regain their position.

If the executives have demonstrably imperilled the business and refuse, or cannot remedy the position, they have to go. This can be costly but essential.

Whatever the outcome, the board should immediately implement the agenda set out in 2 above.

Part Three

EXPERT
PERSPECTIVES

12

Views of PLC institutional shareholders

Most boards in Britain do not have to worry about their shareholders because they and the directors are one and the same
people. Only when outside shareholders are involved is it necessary for the directors to consider other peoples' aims and wishes.

Most directors of small firms only start to learn about shareholder accountability when they seek outside capital. The source
could be private funds but more often it will be from a professional
venture capitalist who will apply his own conditions for participat-
ing in the equity.

It is only when companies are listed on the major exchanges that
boards are required to obey Stock Exchange rules and the
guidelines of the major institutions that own around 70–75% of
British listed companies. These shareholders are there not to run
companies but to see, as far as possible, that their investments
thrive in good times and bad. To do this many institutional
shareholders take considerable trouble to learn about the
companies in which they are invested and the people who run
them. In turn, investors advise the directors of companies what is
expected from them.

Investors rightly ask a lot from their directors and this chapter sets out what major shareholders seek from their investments. There are four sections:

1 The major players and how they work.
2 What they expect from the companies they own.
3 What they expect from non-executive directors.
4 The voice of the professionals.

1 The major players and how they work

The two largest in Britain are the Association of British Insurers (AGI) and the National Association of Pension Funds (NAPF). Together they own about 60% of all quoted companies.

Institutional Shareholders Committee (ISC)

The ISC acts as an umbrella which is used, where appropriate to coordinate the activities of all the investment committees. These include the ABI and NAPF and three others, the Unit Trust Association, the Association of Unit Trust Companies and the British Merchant Banking and Security Houses Association. The ISC forms a powerful group representing some 75% of all company ownership and has a Secretary General whose primary job is to act as a channel of communication with boards of directors.

What powers do the Investment Committees have?

By themselves very little but, in representing members' interests, substantial. By calling an extraordinary General Meeting, the institutions working together can remove any one director, or the entire board should that be necessary. But that is not their way. They see their job not as running British companies but rather to operate behind the scenes to influence board composition and conduct. This guidance is particularly needed when a management style that may have been acceptable in the booming 1980s needs to be modified to cope with the recession of the early 1990s. This is how they see the relationship working:

- Institutions as responsible shareholders want to understand the companies that they own. They recommend shareholders open channels to senior management, learn about corporate objectives, and assess management quality. In return they want to explain the expectations and requirements of shareholders.
- A board would be wise to respond to an approach from shareholders. Not only is this good sense but it may pay future dividends if the board wants support in the event of an unwelcome take-over bid. Where the arguments are finely balanced it is usual for institutions to support managements that they know and trust.
- An institution does not normally wish to be given price sensitive information which debars it from trading. However, there may be occasions when several major shareholders agree to take collective remedial action and as a result are in a privileged position and cannot deal in shares.
- Shareholders become concerned if assets appear to have been sold at something less than their true value and want to see full details of any deals such as management buy-outs. They would also question the management's right to increase borrowing powers without consultation.

The Association of British Insurers (ABI)

The ABI is a trade association representing some 450 members (excluding Lloyds) transacting over £50bn of business in the UK every year; this total represents over 90% of their total activity. The association does not seek to regulate its members but to provide a code of practice and conduct.

In 1989, the insurance industry received £60bn premiums; the majority was for long-term business such as life insurance and pensions. The balance was for general business including property, motor, marine and aircraft insurance.

ABI members invest nearly £275m p.a. – two-thirds being in equity markets which represents some 30% of the total UK stock market capitalization. The association has an Investment Committee of 20 investment managers representing ABI membership. There is also a full-time secretariat to represent the views of the investment committee where appropriate.

The IC does not become involved in matters of investment

judgement but it exists to protect ABI members' interests and to implement decisions on matters of general principle. These might include the rights of shareholders, European Directors, liaising with the Takeover Panel, representation on appropriate CBI and stock exchange committees and the like.

The investment committee also works closely with other investing associations, for example preparing guidelines on matters of general concern to investment managers and directors. These include the Role and Duties of Directors and the Responsibilities of Institutional Shareholders which are of direct interest to directors. All the institutions meet together under the Institutional Shareholders Committee. The work of the secretariat is described in more detail below.

National Association of Pension Funds (NAPF)

The NAPF is the leading organization encouraging employers to establish, develop, and extend pension provision for their employees. The investment committee operates a service aimed at improving the security and efficiency of pension fund investment assets. Assets under NAPF members' control amount to £300bn.

The NAPF's investment committee is involved with similar issues to that of the ABI and they liaise regularly on matters of mutual interest. However, there are significant differences between the perspectives of their institutions, particularly as regards taxation.

The NAPF's investment committee also works to promote its ideas through recommendations, guidelines and codes of conduct, particularly relating to self-investment and performance management. The investment committee also publishes bulletins and books, organizes an annual investment conference and runs seminars.

2 What is expected by investment committees

From time to time the ABI, NAPF and the ISC write papers on behalf of investors to encourage practice which, in the view of the majority shareholders, will stimulate discussion and lead to sound practices. Several have been written in the early 1990s, probably the most significant being that by the Institutional Shareholders Committee of April 18th 1991, 'The Role and Duties of Directors – a Statement of Best Practice'. These documents are important to companies because they underlie institutional thinking; the gist of their recommendations is discussed below.

Structural aspects

- Institutions support unitary boards for Britain where all directors bear equal responsibility. Boards should be operated in accordance with the Companies Acts, the International Stock Exchange Year Book (Yellow Book) and the Takeover Code.
- The institutions recommend the division of the role of chairman and chief executive. This is because if they are combined, there is a possibility of a conflict of interest and too great a concentration of power. Where it is necessary to combine both roles, an independent committee of the board should be appointed to review, when necessary, the performance of the individual.
- Independent directors are an essential feature of the board of most companies and should be of sufficient quantity and calibre for their views to carry significant weight. This is a matter of particular importance when the chairman and chief executive are the same person.
- Companies are recommended to appoint Audit Committees. These are there both to receive information from the auditors and to question the strength of the internal systems. In some companies independent directors are the sole representatives, in others, executives are included.
- It is good practice to appoint independent directors to supervise an activity where a possible conflict of interest may exist with executive directors. For example, this might occur during the buy-out of a subsidiary.
- Institutions are particularly keen that independent directors should be truly independent. This is more likely to be assured if the independent director has not been an executive of the company in the last few years, has not been retained as a professional adviser and is not involved in a significant trading

relationship. He should only have directorships in other companies in the same industry with the approval of the board.

The independent director's role

- The ISC Paper affirms the position that, under Common Law, directors are in a position of trust to the company not just to the shareholders. They should act in the best interest of the business and not place themselves in conflict by making a secret profit out of a transaction or contract. If directors are negligent, third parties can sue both the company and the individuals.
- Directors must exercise whatever skill they may have and exercise reasonable care. This rather bland description is at odds with the much more stringent requirements of Section 213 and 214 of the Insolvency Act (see Chapter 8).
- The 1985 Companies Act provides additional requirements. For example, shareholders must give their approval before directors can be involved in property transactions (above £50,000). The Act also requires a company to disclose loans made to a director.
- Directors are required to disclose immediately any acquisitions or disposals under the control of them or their family; the Company Secretary than has immediately to inform the Stock Exchange. The 1985 Act also prohibits any dealing when the director (or any other individual) is in possession of price sensitive information. This means an absolute bar on making transactions within two months prior to publication of interim or final accounts.
- Independent directors should acknowledge a particular duty to monitor the performance of the board as a whole. They should report to the shareholders if reasonable efforts have not removed the causes of their dissatisfaction.

The appointment

- Directors' service contracts should not exceed three years. They must be approved by shareholders, be available for scrutiny at the registered office and at the AGM.
- The appointment of any new director terminates automatically

at the next AGM when directors can offer themselves for re-election. The paper recommends that the Articles should stipulate that one-third of the directors should retire by rotation every year and, should they so wish, offer themselves for re-election.

- The Articles should provide that a director may be removed from office by written resolution of at least 75% of the directors, to be confirmed at the next AGM. The Articles should also provide for a director's dismissal if he fails to attend a specific number of board meetings.
- The paper recommends that the Articles place a limit on a director's remuneration and that it should be considered by the Remuneration Committee composed of independent directors. Details of any performance-linked schemes should be disclosed in the annual accounts.
- Independent directors should not be offered participation in share option plans and should not be eligible for compensation for loss of office. It is becoming more usual for independent directors to have a fixed span of service.

3 What is expected of non-executive directors

Technically, all directors have equal responsibility but it is the job of the executives to propose and implement policy under the general direction of the board. The independent directors are there to contribute to, and question, executive proposals and decisions; they should also monitor performance.

There are two fundamental roles for independent directors:

- To be part of a team contributing to the collective work of the board by supplying both specialized and general business acumen to the board's decisions. A good independent director should be able to add a strategic dimension to the board's thinking and to challenge assumptions if this is necessary. He should also be available to any executive director or chairman to act as a sounding board.
- An independent director is also there to see that the administration is sound, and that adequate monitoring systems are in place through audit and other committees (see Chapter 2). This role

is not a sinecure. An independent director should make it his business to understand how the company is run, who has authority for moving cash, be satisfied that working capital is correctly stated and insist that the board is provided with full, timely and accurate information. He should know what is going on.

4   The voice of the professionals

Mike Sandland, Chief Investment Manager of the Norwich Union and Chairman of the ISC

Mike Sandland believes that it is important that the institutions should be involved in the current debate on corporate governance and how it should develop. In the past, institutions could look the other way and sell their holdings; but this is no longer possible with the weight of equities held in relatively few hands. The institutions now have to enter the debate on what shareholder responsibility means and how this should be discharged.

This change has been brought about in three ways:

- The institutions have become progressively larger holders of British equities.
- The institutions have become much more aware of their responsibilities as owners.
- This responsibility has been sharpened by the 1990–1 recession which has thrown up a number of weaknesses that were generated in the good times. It is as if the flood tide of the 1980s is now ebbing leaving some disagreeable flotsam on the beach.

The institutions seem to have perceived the more puritanical mood of the 1990s rather faster than their industrial counterparts. For example, the institutions perceived quite quickly the public outcry that would follow companies awarding their senior executives large salary and bonus payments. Most institutions like their influence to be felt primarily behind the scenes where a chairman or chief executive can be removed without a great stir. If a public confrontation occurs, both sides will consider their media image.

Sandland believes that the April 1991 ISC declaration of best practice sets out sound basic principles for the conduct and behaviour of independent directors. The document also puts an onus on the institutions to make a sensible response to an independent director who has gone through the correct boardroom procedure of voicing a disquiet about policy or procedures.

The institutions, however, still have to come to terms with independent director involvement. On the one hand shareholders want them to make a major contribution to their board, taking part in the committees, involving themselves in strategy and learning about the business. All this is costly for the right person and Sandlands would be the first to agree that independent directors should be properly compensated. On the other hand, the ISC wants independent directors to retain their independence which could be prejudiced by high levels of remuneration. Perhaps there is a requirement for a sort of professional independent director who is paid handsomely by a carefully picked number of companies.

Richard Regen, Secretary to the ABI's Investment Committee

The ABI's investment committee is the forum for discussing matters of continuing interest to its members. It meets formally once a month and, in addition, will consider individual requests for adjudication. For example, a company might wish to change its Articles of Association which might affect shareholders' rights. The investment committee may also be approached on other matters such as executive share option plans or remuneration packages. It is clearly better for the company to raise the matter privately rather than publish a proposal only to suffer a public rebuff.

Early warning of company difficulties may come through either individual investors or an approach by non-executive directors. Here it is usual to form a 'small case' committee (possibly with other investment committees) to outline a solution that can be implemented by the ABI secretariat. Among the required remedies may be the need to strengthen the board, for example, by the appointment of a finance director or by separating the roles of the chairman and chief executive.

Another requirement may be for the board to appoint additional independent directors. In other cases, the groups may require certain directors to be removed. On some occasions the small case committee members will be prepared to become insiders (thus forbidden to deal) by receiving price-sensitive information in order to resolve a problem satisfactorily.

Clive Gilchrist, Chairman of the NAPF Investment Committee

The investment committee's primary role is to prevent wealth destruction. It does this by influencing companies in which its members have an investment either singly or with other investment committees. The NAPF sees itself as a pro-active catalyst learning from company managements about their aims and objectives; and in turn, telling them about how pension fund managements view their investments. The investment committee believes that the institutions should work more closely with the banks, although this liaison does not work as well as it might.

Clive Gilchrist explains that his committee becomes involved with a company when requested by one or more of its members. Initially, the information is non-confidential and is sourced either directly from their own analysts, through the City, press reports or direct meetings. When the investment committee takes a view on an issue – often in association with the ABI or the ISC – it communicates this to members who are free to act independently. The NAPF does not wield a block vote. NAPF members do not like to be prevented from dealing by becoming insiders, if this can be avoided, though ad hoc groups are sometimes set up to act on a confidential matter.

The NAPF is a firm believer in the role of independent directors and has referred a number of companies to Pro Ned. It would like to see more senior executives giving up their time to act as independent directors in other companies to strengthen the UK's industrial base. Gilchrist believes that independent directors can be particularly influential on board committees and should be determined to act independently, even if in a minority of one. The latest ISC paper makes it easier for any independent director to raise problems with a shareholder after having stated his discontent at the board table.

Finally, the views of a prominent institutional investor:

John Reeve, Chief Executive of Sun Life Assurance Ltd

Sun Life, like other major institutions, has shareholdings in many different companies and finds the present monitoring methods rather cumbersome. Reeve is in full agreement with the aims of the ISC paper, particularly on the appointment of competent independent directors and their contribution to board committees.

John Reeve believes that independent directors really come into their own during some untoward event. This might be a financial crisis, a take-over, a management failure or a disagreement on major strategic issues. Many investors hold quite unrealistic expectations of what an independent director can be expected to achieve. It is impossible for someone only involved a day or two a month, to contribute to anything other than the major factors affecting the business.

The whole question of corporate governance is touched by the so-called Fifth Directive from the EC Commission. Certainly, independent directors have a significant role in the way companies are run. However, the 'Holy Grail' of shareholder/company relations has yet to be discovered.

13

Views of investment and venture capitalists

There are well over 400,000 private companies that are largely unknown to the conventional investing institutions. This is the territory of 3i and the other venture capitalists who are providing capital and dealing first hand with individuals who are both majority shareholders and managers. Generally the linkage between investors and their clients is closer than for the major institutions investing in quoted companies. As part of their arrangements, venture capitalists expect to require and receive regular monthly information.

Venture capitalists grew in prominence during the 1970s and 1980s catering for start-ups, management buy-out (MBOs) and management buy-in (MBIs), as well as for requirements for development capital.

The close relationship between a private company and its institutional investor makes for a more intense atmosphere than in a PLC. The timeframe and the emphasis on cash generation present special problems both for the venture capitalists and for the independent directors they often wish to appoint. The individual appointed must be acceptable both to the venture capitalist and to the majority shareholders, and he often forms a link between the two. Frequently, part of the function is to fill gaps in the skills and experience of the executive team.

This chapter includes contributions from a number of the UK's most senior investment capital practitioners.

British Venture Capital Association

The umbrella organization for venture capitalists is the British Venture Capital Association (BVCA) whose members in 1990 invested £1.4bn in 1,559 companies. Management buy-outs or buy-ins accounted for 52% of the invested cash or 26% by number, start-ups for 12% of the cash or 26% by number, and the balance for expansion and secondary purchase. Over one-third of all finance was invested in consumer related businesses and a further fifth was technology related.

Some of the 122 BVCA members are also ISC members (see Chapter 12) and others are subsidiaries of British and foreign clearing banks. However, the majority are specialists in private company investment, led by 3i. 3i is the most experienced practitioner in this type of investment in Britain (and probably the world) having started in 1945 with the support of the Bank of England and the major clearing banks.

If a private company equity investment is to proceed, most venture capitalists will require the appointment of an independent director or chairman. This is needed because most executives involved in buy-outs have little direct experience of dealing with people outside their businesses, notably banks, shareholders and perhaps government departments. The experiences of independent directors working in this field vary widely. For example, some situations call for all-round experience; others need specific skills related to an industry, technology or marketing.

The requirements also vary between investors. For example, 3i places its own employees on investee boards only when involved in a syndicated transaction with other institutions (where difficulties could arise if 3i behaved differently from the other investors). Most other institutions normally arrange for an outside chairman or independent director and also place one of their own executives on the board, to represent the interests of the institution.

An independent director or chairman of a venture capital

backed company has exactly the same legal responsibilities as those of a PLC. The work has considerable intensity and there is a major difference of style. For example, most small companies will not have board committees, such as audit and remuneration committees as required by the institutional shareholders for PLCs. Also on occasion, an immediate problem may demand the concentrated and personal hands-on attention of an independent director.

Any independent director appointed to a small company should make careful enquiries before accepting the position. For example, he would be wise to question the auditors concerning the valuation of the working capital and the soundness of the recording systems. If these are not satisfactory, an independent director could be well advised to see that the position was rectified – if necessary requiring a prior investigation before joining the board.

This is how a number of senior venture capitalists operate and what they seek from independent directors.

Derek Sach, Former Group Managing Director, 3i PLC

In 1991, 3i had some £2bn invested in 4,000 customers in the UK. Although business declined somewhat since 1989 it was still doing around 50% of all transactions in Britain and 20% of the value. To some extent the fall reflects the perception that perhaps some of the business written in the late 1980s was overpriced.

Unlike some venture capitalists, 3i is a long-term investor holding its stakes over many years; for this reason, it sees itself as provider of investment capital (rather than of venture capital, an expression which tends to be associated with short-term involvement in high growth early stage companies).

In addition to financial expertise, 3i has an Industry Department based at Solihull staffed with senior industrial executives, both general management and financial, who provide an industrial input to investment decisions. 3i believes it is unique in having such an in-house resource, which gives it an unusually well-informed insight into the managerial, market, technical, industrial and human aspects of a company's situation and prospects. It has also built up a considerable resource of independent directors (see Chapter 4).

3i operates from 24 branch offices in the UK, each headed by a local director. Under direction, an investment executive (the 'investment controller' or simply 'controller') is assigned to each vetted enquiry; to assess the size, prospects, and degree of risk of the proposition. If the potential risk/return looks satisfactory, the controller will then formulate and negotiate a financing package acceptable to both sides which will need to be cleared with his local director. At some point the controller may wish to involve the Industry Department if the proposed investment is specialized, complex or above average risk.

If an equity investment is to proceed, 3i will frequently require the appointment of an independent director or chairman whose job is to balance the skills around the board table. This is an important task because in many situations (management buy-outs for example), the directors may have little direct experience of running an autonomous company, or of dealing with banks, shareholders or government departments.

3i seeks to ensure that for every investment there is in position a management team and a board adequate for the size and nature of the business. For example, a start-up might need one entrepreneur, one other manager plus some financial input; the board might then need one independent director to add broad business experience. However, when a company reaches a turnover of perhaps £10m, there is a need for a more formal structure, and a broader team.

The spread of 3i business includes many start-ups, buy-outs and buy-ins and almost invariably there is a chief executive in place (often in his early 40s). The most usual gap is the finance function, which often leads to the appointment of a suitably experienced independent director, although this should never be a substitute for an accounting executive. The other main gap can be for an independent chairman to take the place of an experienced senior executive who would be present in many organizations – described by 3i as having 'grey hairs' around.

The primary aim of the chairman is to bring general business knowledge to a board that might otherwise only possess narrowly defined skills. In addition, specific knowledge could be useful. Thus, a company in the defence industry might benefit from a chairman who knew his way around the MOD and procurement procedures. However, if the company made industrial fasteners, general experience in light engineering and in the company's market might be valuable. All depends on the balance of skills and experience already at the board table. It is probably a mistake for a company to appoint a chairman for his contacts, although this is sometimes desired by the company.

Apart from a few specific instances, 3i does not appoint any of its own staff to a board believing that outside directors should be independent. Another reason is that problems can arise when a 3i employee is appointed to a board and then finds himself at odds with another 3i employee acting for 3i as investor. For example, if an appointee was finance director, needing to raise further cash, he could be at odds with a 3i executive taking a different view.

A further reason is that many individuals recruited and trained to make investment appraisals, recommendations and then manage the ongoing relationship, may not make particularly good independent directors. They may neither have the expertise nor management exposure to make a general contribution to board discussions. Later on, when they have more experience, they may make excellent directors, but not initially. This fits in with 3i's view that it is preferable to keep the role of investor separate from that of running the company; thus 3i does not set out to be a hands-on investor, preferring to aim for 'controlled involvement'.

When 3i nominates a chairman, an individual is recommended to the company who will bring with him a broad perspective of the industry and experience of being able to make a board work effectively. The person should spend some time with the company and get to know the people to ensure that all the aims are compatible.

When a chairman or independent director is introduced, this normally happens after the deal is completed, except in rare cases when the role is fundamental to a successful contract. To emphasize further independence, 3i does not normally require that the chairman becomes a shareholder alongside 3i. In the long run, an individual's reputation is probably more important than any gain derived from a shareholding.

Once a board has been appointed, the directors should ensure that management produces competent monthly accounts which are then copied to the investors. In due course, the chairman also initiates the appropriate actions towards the report and accounts and the AGM.

When an independent director is appointed, 3i expects him to ensure that the board establishes appropriate arrangements to handle all investor relations, including that with 3i. This often has the virtue of keeping an informal supplementary channel open between the independent director and the investors. More direct contact is not normally required, that is until things start to go wrong. An independent director's prime objective should be to help put the company back on the rails – resignation being the last alternative.

A company in trouble almost invariably needs a change of management if new money is to be provided ('something has to change'). Executive changes can generally be organized through the chairman, but there is a difficulty if the problem lies in a director who is also a major shareholder. 3i takes the view that shareholders have a right to go bust if that is their wish; hence if the company is to be saved, the individual may have to be bought out. If the chairman needs changing, 3i often has to intervene directly.

Syndicated investments can present special difficulties because often the various investors are pulling in different directions. Some who took large equity stakes in the 1980s found themselves inadequately trained in problem solving. The difficulties were compounded when the banks, particularly UK subsidiaries of foreign banks, took excessive loan positions. Now in the early 1990s there is a reversion towards equity finance and the retirement of debt. 3i has generally received a helpful response from UK based banks when addressing the affairs of companies in difficulty.

Richard Hargreaves, Chief Executive, Baronsmead

Baronsmead tends to focus on the smaller end of of the venture capital market with investments of between £0.25m and £1.5m. Most of its investments are established companies or buy- outs where the individuals have a good knowledge of the business but may need an outsider to take them through a growth stage.

To assist in the development of the company, Baronsmead often insists on an independent chairman being appointed to form a bridge between the management and shareholders. He should not represent either camp and must be acceptable to both parties. These are the basic qualifications:

- Knows something of the industry with its associated opportunities and pitfalls
- Be capable of running the corporate process efficiently
- Can make a contribution, not just earn a fee.

In addition, Baronsmead often seeks the appointment of a financially trained director who brings corporate finance skills and generally represents the 'money'. The executives prepare the monthly information pack and are responsible for day-to-day communication with the investors and banks. The chairman is only expected to perform this communication function on statutory occasions.

The position changes when things 'start hitting rocks in the water' – too many financiers pulling in different directions is a recipe for a disaster. This is true of both venture capitalists and banks. In an ideal situation a company should have just one bank and not more than two venture capitalists who can work well together, sharing a common philosophy and outlook.

Baronsmead has difficulty in finding a chairman who is precisely right for each business. In the main, appointments are made from direct contacts or strong recommendations which tend to be more successful than introductions from cold-calling letters and advertisements.

In general, veterans of the venture capital industry do not have a high opinion of independent directors. This observation has focused Baronsmead's attention on finding the right types of individual to meet the needs of their businesses. There are a host of people who would like to become independent directors, but many of those from larger companies do not understand, for example, the part cash plays in the operations of a small company. Furthermore, accountants have not proved all that helpful in this field because they lack specific industrial experience.

Turnround specialists have their place as a sub-set of the whole, but their training is not to grow businesses but to wring-out costs. Seldom are they strong at working out growth strategies, introducing staff development etc.

Baronsmead's investment philosophy is to put its skill and expertise (and that of others) into an enterprise and to harvest the capital gain through a sale, not a flotation. It takes considerable trouble to inform the management team and the chairman of its intentions so that everyone understands the investment goals. At the outset, the chairman is given all the information that is available about the business and every chance to talk to the management and to investigate matters for himself.

Once the business plan has been agreed, Baronsmead ask for a yearly meeting to keep up to date with progress to learn of future objectives and plans. In addition, the management is invited quarterly to discuss progress with the outside investors.

When businesses go wrong, they invariably need more cash and a change in management. In Baronsmead's view, the first rescue responsibility falls to the venture capitalist; any accommodation by the banks such as converting fixed to variable costs should be secondary – and only after the business is up and running once more.

A rescue example

One company that was running out of cash needed a new chairman and an injection of funds. The addition of equity meant that Baronsmead held a majority shareholding alongside the new chairman. The managers recognized that the chairman held a majority proxy, but it was understood that this would only be used after prior consultation with the other investors.

Baronsmead have taken pressure off the chairman by taking upon themselves certain difficult decisions such as cutting the board's salaries. Others might follow such as dismissing particular directors even though they might be significant shareholders.

Patrick Dunne, Investment Director, 3i PLC

3i's investment activities described by Derek Sach rely for their independent directors on what might be described as an 'in-house Pro Ned'. Individuals are classified according to their skills and listed on a central register (see Chapter 4).

To become a member, prospective independent directors should have served on boards with outside shareholders – this excludes some potentially excellent directors, but life in a small or medium independent company tends to raise different problems and can be heavily involved with relationships with external sources of finance. Experience also shows that some directors who have served successfully in large companies may find it difficult to adjust to the very different environment of smaller businesses.

Unlike independent directors in listed companies, 3i is often seeking to add industrial or functional skills. Investors in private companies are sometimes criticized for this stance, but the appointment has to satisfy several parties – not least the majority shareholders who are often themselves executive directors. Whatever the director's skills, independent directors are chosen with regard to the needs of the company and shareholders as a whole.

As Derek Sach explains, when a chairman or independent director is appointed, this normally follows completion of the deal and the individual is chosen after consultation between the 3i investment controller and the board. Ideally he should know the individual candidates personally but, if further names are needed for the shortlist, he consults the central register.

When a business goes wrong, 3i (usually as a minority shareholder) cannot exercise the same degree of control as major institutions with a quoted company, but does have the advantage of being close to the business through monthly reports. Another advantage is that 3i has a large spread of investments, some 4,000 in UK. If, for example, computer retailers in the home counties are finding trade difficult then other investments in the industry can be checked.

If problems are seen to be caused by a management weakness, 3i might wish to appoint a strong independent director to help steer the company through a crisis; in more extreme cases a company doctor could be introduced. Coincidental with the appointment, the investment executive would bring together the people closest to the company such as the bankers, the auditors, independent directors and executives to agree the position and subsequent action.

Allan Speirs, Director, Advent

Advent Ltd is part of the Advent International Network of independently managed partnerships operating in 16 different companies with a spread of international shareholding and total investments of $1.6bn. Advent has been active in the UK for 10 years specializing in technology-based sectors of industry; some of its portfolio companies have been early stage investments, some are later stage and buy-out financings. There are also some small listed companies. The range of deals in the UK varies from £0.25m to £4m with an average of around £1m.

During 1990–1 with the capital markets drying up in Britain, Advent focused on trade buyers to harvest their investments. Timing can be difficult in a technology business when rapidly changing product life cycles enforce a shorter time involvement than the normal average five years. This is generally accepted by a young management which understands the market dynamics and is prepared to move around much more than was usual 15 years ago.

When making an investment, Advent will appoint one of its staff to the board as their representative, and also an outside chairman. The roles are quite distinct. The chairman is there to act as a bridge between the company and shareholders, to ensure that the board is efficiently run and the executive team remains competent. Unlike Baronsmead, the chairman is not normally a shareholder. He is recruited from a number of contacts with the occasional use of head-hunters.

An Advent-appointed independent director will have industrial experience; he is there to work with the company, not as Advent's representative. Advent caters for the potentially conflicting roles of chairman and nominated independent director by keeping the functions distinct and separate.

In the event of losses, cash or other problems, the rapport built up between the chief executive and Advent's nominee is extremely important. This channel is essential if both parties are to steer the company through a rough patch – most of the contact being outside the board room. In addition, Advent will bring in someone else, typically with a financial background from within their own team to appraise the situation. This may lead to new financing if the business can be salvaged.

Like Baronsmead, Advent tries to ensure that any syndication is with investors (both the company and the executive) having a similar attitude to their own. Any refinancing package should include the banks who are encouraged to convert short- to long-term debt or some of the debt into equity.

14

Views of experienced independent directors

This chapter presents the views of a group of experienced independent directors from large PLCs to buy-outs and start-ups. It begins with a summary for each main category of company and while there are many common features, there are also important differences. It then sets out each director's position in more detail.

Summary for the director of a PLC

These are some of the more important issues raised in discussion:

- Time spent in reconnaissance is seldom wasted. Companies seeking an independent director will thoroughly vet prospective candidates and the individual should do his homework too (see Chapter 6). The interviews could be searching and take time but it is time well spent. If an appointment term is for three or less years, this should not be a matter for concern. It is the modern practice and there is often a good chance of renewal.

- A thorough induction procedure is essential and should be used to test some of the assessments made beforehand. Details of board committees should be established – there may be an invitation to sit on at least one of them.
- It is important to understand how the board works and the relationship between chairman, the executives and independent directors. This should extend to cover how meetings are conducted and the time spent on reviewing past performance compared with discussions on strategy or policy.
- If needed, independent directors should be prepared to initiate action to fire the chief executive or chairman. This requires high diplomatic skills to gain a majority around the board table, and if necessary obtaining the support of the shareholders or bankers.
- The ideal board of a smaller company should comprise the chairman, chief executive, finance director and a majority of independent directors.
- It is risky to join any board where the majority consists of time-serving executives. They may be more concerned to protect their pensions, than to take the business forward.
- Specific expertise can, on occasion, greatly assist the working of the board. It might for example be on one of the board committees or in helping with strategic thinking.
- Board reports and monthly financial statements should not be assumed to be reliable and in any case may exclude important aspects. If in doubt, independent directors should be advised to devise their own indicator through contacts with managers, customer meetings with salesmen or trade contacts.

Summary for the director of a private company

- Those who understand or have direct experience of the business will usually be able to make the most rapid contribution. Prior knowledge can bring contacts, a 'nose' for the most significant issues and saves explanation time. It is helpful to learn rapidly the three or four critical factors that drive added value and make for success or failure.
- By the time a problem hits the operating statement, it could be too late. Board papers should concentrate not only on monthly profit and loss accounts, balance sheet, and lending covenants

but on leading indicators. Experienced independent directors can help the board work out their own advanced signals.

- A major priority is to learn the chief executive's strengths and weaknesses and gain his confidence by understanding his problems or constraints. Where he is also a major shareholder trust generally precedes influence.
- When joining a board, an independent director is wise to concentrate on an area of personal expertise before moving on to contribute on a broader front. While each board member carries the same responsibility, the independent directors have a prime role in being sensitive to external factors.
- Independent directors should understand the objectives of banks and venture capitalists who should be kept closely in touch with progress. It is sensible to learn their aspirations and try to seek common aims with them and around the board table.
- Investors and banks will not necessarily all take the same view if things go wrong, particularly if the investment is syndicated. Investment executives and bank managers can change so it is wise to ensure contact is maintained at a senior level.
- The best background for a venture capital independent director is often general management experience in a similar business to the company. A directorship should never be taken 'just for the money', the director must have the courage to speak out without fear of being fired.
- If necessary, an independent director must be prepared to assume executive responsibility.

These are some of the qualities either expressed or exhibited by the individuals interviewed:

- *Intellect*. An independent director must be able to keep up and contribute to board discussion.
- *Courage*. There are times when an independent director has to question his colleagues around the board table without fear of isolation. It is better to state a position on a major issue and be asked to resign than to compromise with a deeply felt judgement.
- *Curiosity*. Almost all businesses are stimulating and being a member of a board is an opportunity to learn from the activity and from one's colleagues.
- *Empathy*. There is little point in being a member of a board, however powerful the contribution, unless an individual is

prepared to make a point in a manner that is acceptable to his colleagues.

- *Numeracy*. Members of a board should not only understand the basics of financial accounting but be able to search behind the figures to understand their meaning.
- *Imagination*. There should be at least some directors who have the imagination to visualize the potential for a business and be able to express this in practical terms.

The following individuals have kindly given of their time to express their ideas:

Eric Barton, Director, 3i and in Large Syndicated Buyouts

Background: joined 3i as a graduate trainee in 1968 and after five years in 3i's regional investment team, joined 3i Corporate Finance in 1973 which involved buying and selling companies and advising listed companies on new issues.

Since 1980 Barton has been involved in corporate transactions including 3i's largest investment in support of the £2.2bn bid for Gateway by Isosceles – still the biggest UK buy-out. Since 1990 he has been concentrating as an independent director in circumstances where 3i have a major investment.

Normally 3i does not nominate staff to represent 3i directly on boards. There are, however, two occasions when an appointment is considered:

- When larger investments are syndicated with another institution and 3i is the lead investor. In these cases a senior 3i director will often be appointed to discharge a responsibility on behalf of the syndicate as a whole.
- In a joint venture situation or a syndication where 3i is not leading. The collective style of the investors may require each to nominate its own director, in which case 3i will often fall in with the general practice.

In the former case, the 3i nominee has a responsibility to see that a strong board of executive and independent directors is appointed, to see that the board is working well and that there is a good shareholder liaison.

In most cases, the institutional nominee's work is done when the company is floated or the investment realized so that the institutions have achieved marketability for their shareholding. However, other independent directors introduced by 3i for their industrial knowledge and contacts may well continue with the company. Barton therefore sees his role as transitory – guiding the company to achieve the shareholder's objectives within an acceptable time scale.

A further essential factor in 3i's thinking is compliance with the Securities and Investment Board and like regulations. Any member of 3i staff with a board appointment should have his first responsibility to the company itself and should not be involved in 3i's investment decisions. Eric Barton emphasizes this division of responsibility as he has seen too many boardroom wrangles over investment decisions, matters which have no place at the board table.

Company familiarization

Familiarization should not be a major problem for the nominee director of the investment capitalist; his institution will have carried out a comprehensive investigation with due diligence and should be able to provide a full briefing. The details will include shareholder expectations, gearing, management incentive packages etc.

Where possible, the investor's nominee should be appointed as soon as possible after the deal has been concluded. The negotiations should have built up respect between the parties including the need to create a balanced board of executive and independent directors. Barton believes that mistakes are made because people have been appointed to a board without first creating a working relationship; this has lead to tensions, particularly with executives who have not been used to dealing with independent directors.

Part of the nominee director's job is to judge the strengths and weaknesses of the buy-out team and to complement these with appropriate independent directors. Some who are administratively strong may need an outsider who is marketing orientated. Others who are market driven are likely to need financial support.

A frequent source of much soul-searching is whether an independent chairman should be appointed. Barton joins the investing institutions in believing that the role of chairman and chief executive should be separated when shares are widely held. The roles are quite different and this position is often accepted even by headstrong chief executives. Clearly the relationship between chairman and chief executive is very important and the 'chemistry' must work well.

Joining a board

A new independent director should work out a joining plan in conjunction with the chairman and chief executive shortly after appointment. This is an important issue because after a suitable induction period he will be deemed to have satisfied himself that the company is run with due care and integrity. Among other matters, the independent director may wish to:

- Learn about the company's history and background; visit the principal sites and ensure he meets the divisional managers and middle management as soon as possible after joining the board. A good move could be to persuade the board to meet at each company/divisional site in turn and suggest that presentations should be made to the board. This would give the directors a chance to know more about the business and be seen by employees.
- Find out what drives added value, whether this lies in product design, a production process, market strength etc. Ask the executives about their own preferred leading indicators on the strength of the market place, sales trends etc.
- Understand the nature of the market, is it open and fiercely competitive or structured with barriers to entry – technological or regulatory?
- Understand the financial position by discussing the board reports with the finance director. Usually it is soon apparent whether he is content to produce print-outs or seeks genuinely to understand and communicate the commercial and financial dynamics of the business. One particular issue is whether the management information package adequately reports on the cash position and outlook – essential in a leveraged buy-out; also does the pack report on the company's performance against the banks' borrowing covenants.
- Meet the auditors after reading several years' report and accounts. It is wise always to insist on reading their management letters.
- Understand buy-out documentation including the shareholders agreement and special rights reserved to the independent directors.
- Consider how the company prepares its strategic plan. Is this a matter of adding 10% to last year's budget or a genuine attempt to plan for (at least) the next year; and how does this relate to any agreed exit for the shareholders?
- Establish what programme of board meetings is planned, where are they to be held and how far in advance are the board papers to be available. An independent director should insist that the

documents are complete, and not dribbled out during the board meeting.

Board meetings

Venture capitalists and banks will insist on receiving well-presented, accurate and timely board information as a condition of providing buyout finance. This invariably includes:

- Monthly operating statements and balance sheets.
- Cashflow projections showing expected headroom in bank facilities several months ahead.
- Important banking covenants such as interest cover and net worth ratios.

It is essential that the board of a leveraged business puts high priority on cash generation. Timing is essential for a buy-out and the board must have a contingency plan to generate cash if the assumptions in the plan are no longer valid.

Serious conflicts can arise between the various investing institutions and banks, particularly if the programme is lagging behind the plan. The responsibility for handling such conflicts is primarily the chairman's but each independent director should be familiar with the expectations of the various parties and ensure that these are also understood by the executives.

The job of an independent director on a PLC

A director of a PLC is more concerned that the company's policies do not overextend the balance sheet. There is a balance between the executives who know and run the business and the independent directors who should have the acumen and courage to speak out and challenge actions that could prove a disaster.

In some cases, speaking out may not be enough, independent directors may sometimes have to take control. These are some of the matters to be considered:

- What is the company's strategy? An independent director should ensure that the corporate plan is made for at least one year ahead, more often three to five. Once agreed, progress is considered at least every other month.
- The 1986 Insolvency Act applies pressures and calls for skills that were not mentioned under common law. The board must debate any issue of possible wrongful trading and come to a sensible view of

the commercial realities which should be recorded for later scrutiny, if needed.

Independent director attributes

Ideally, independent directors should work in teams, not in isolation. While it is helpful to have some experience in the relevant industry, breadth of vision is essential. An investment background can be limiting if it concentrates purely on the left-hand side of the balance sheet and shareholder perceptions.

The best background for an independent director is probably through the general management route, then with extensive experience in a range of different situations. The best prospect is someone who is financially independent, is not looking for a job, but is attracted by the situation. Independent directors should have personality and courage and be capable of working alongside executives – but not taking over their job unless they are forced to do so.

Barton believes that big company executives can be too powerful for the smaller company and can also find it difficult to cope with the lack of support systems. Some have almost an excess of intellect which might not suit the intense atmosphere of a buy-out preparing for a flotation. Some executives who are encouraged to end their career by becoming independent directors lose touch by leaving the mainstream too quickly, despite having over 10 years of potential contribution ahead of them.

Sir Max Williams, ex Senior Partner of Clifford Chance

Sir Max is former President of the Law Society, a director of Royal Assurance, 3i, and the London Stock Exchange and Chairman of the Review Board of government contracts.

Commitee work

Boards need independent directors who can give not only the appearance, but also the reality, of independence. Independent directors should also be the sole members of the audit and compliance board committees where they must have confidential access to the appropriate officers and external auditors. Each group should be chaired by a senior independent director and meet regularly during the year at intervals reflecting the size and needs of the business. Independent directors should also be involved in other board committee work such as the remuneration or pension committees.

Strategy is also an important area for independent director contribution and they should be present when proposals are discussed in detail. At 3i, for example, the board spends two days a year away from the office to discuss in detail papers prepared by the executives. The decisions can then be formally agreed at a board meeting.

Effective use of independent directors

A wise chairman will make the most effective use of independent directors in sub-committees, not only at board meetings where there is limited time available. A good chairman should have made judgements on where each director can make his particular contribution and will ensure that these are noted by the executives.

The independent directors should become aware of any serious falling off in executive performance and make their views known to the chairman. If the chairman disagrees and the independent directors still feel strongly, they should ask for a private meeting and, if necessary, have their concerns minuted. They may also feel the need to approach the shareholders if no action is forthcoming. If the independent directors believe that the chairman himself is no longer capable then they as a group should approach him directly with their observations.

John Gillum, independent director and non-executive chairman

John Gillum was a director of Kleinwort Benson, head of corporate finance at Samuel Montagu, and with N M Rothschild until his retirement from the City. His first outside directorship was on the board of Wolverhampton Diecasting Company, when his mentor advised him to say nothing for the first two meetings.

Subsequent to WDC he has been an independent director on the boards of Woodhall Trust, Debenhams, Lifeguard Assurance, H Samuel (now Ratners), Sketchley (chairman for five months' bridging period of change), Blagdan Industries (chairman for three years) and Atlantic Computers (as chairman, from the sudden death of the founder until its acquisition).

Company assessment

If approached to join a board then an examination of the company is essential, before any meeting takes place. If there has been a professional relationship then a considerable amount is known about the people and the operations; if little is known, then a contact with a City background can discreetly consult bankers, auditors, lawyers stockbrokers etc. Without direct City connections an individual can still consult such sources as Companies House, trade catalogues and credit references.

Whatever approach is used, it should avoid the potentially embarrassing situation of holding a meeting and then having to back off because of an adverse report. Overall, a mixture of caution, investigation, own judgement and practicality is needed in that sequence.

When a meeting with the chairman or chief executive eventually occurs, it is essential to judge whether the business is run with competence, reliability and integrity; it is also important that the individual can work with the rest of the board. Conversely, the directors have to decide whether they can work with the individual. This is generally a slow process unless there is an emergency calling for rapid action.

Board meetings

Regular board meetings represent a discipline on the executives; they report their stewardship of the business which the independent directors have the opportunity to question. All directors have a right to expect that the information set before them is accurate and timely. This expectation is not always realized, however. Gillum has needed clairvoyance to see through some of the papers presented to him – mainly from companies started by a first generation entrepreneur. The process of examination may be resented; but the board represents a forum, sometimes like a bullfight, when the executives' stewardship is scrutinized.

Gillum believes that the executive directors should be responsible for proposing future strategy which can then be debated by the whole board. For the independent directors to create a policy for executive implementation is a clear recipe for disaster. Forward planning is essential even though it may not seem exciting in the eyes of the City. For example, it may well be right for a retailer to have a policy of opening new shops in prime sites despite the sharper excitement of pursuing an acquisition programme.

Replacing directors

On the downside, there are limits to the amount of goading a chief executive can take without the rest of the board concluding that he should be replaced. Serious questioning about the performance of a division or the suitability of individuals is one matter; attempting to run the company from the board table with the chief executive as a puppet is another.

In simple terms, an independent director is there to underwrite the work of the chief executive. If, however, the confidence is misplaced, the independent director's task is to find a person to do the job better either from within or outside. This can precipitate a crisis which may require the help of shareholders for its resolution. Either the executive goes or the independent director.

Dealing with an underperforming chairman is another matter; he is chairman by consent of the board as a whole and can therefore be removed by his colleagues. If independent director(s) doubt the chairman's competence then it is a question of ascertaining whether there is a consensus for change among the directors. If there is, then the individual must be approached with the board's backing – the shareholders may not be involved. If, however the roles of chairman and chief executive are combined then the board should act as for the chief executive.

Peter Benton, Director General, British Institute of Management

After a background including Unilever and McKinsey, Peter Benton headed the engineering division of Gallaghers and later became Deputy Chairman. Since then he has been Managing Director of BT and Director General of the British Institute of Management, and has held several chairman and board positions.

An independent director's greatest contribution is to be a dispassionate friend to the chief executive and to relay to him the reality of the organization as seen by an outsider. Benton is no great believer in board meetings reviewing progress – you can't steer a ship by gazing at the wake. The board is best employed in creating strategy and watching leading indicators.

Bureaucrats are the enemy of achievement

A number of companies can only operate when in a stable environment; that is, they can only operate within the managed economy that is present in many western nations. Disaster strikes when the previously cosy assumptions are overturned and the business has to adapt to new circumstances. A company is doomed to decline if it has time-serving bureaucrats, not achievers, at each level of the organization. Benton's views are expressed in his book *Riding the Whirlwind* (see References).

The real cutting edge of any company is how the customer perceives the business. When joining a board, Benton insists on spending a day with a salesman to observe how the individual relates to the customer, whether the individual helps to add value, makes an honest case and is regarded as a valued friend.

Whenever he has run a business, Benton spent much of his time meeting and interviewing people at each level in the organization; this is to ensure that, so far as possible, achievers were appointed at every level.

Early warning systems

There is no point in being present at monthly board meetings if all that happens is that the directors are fed with the traditional financial statements included in the board pack. In determining a strategy, each board has to decide not only the forward policy but the leading indicators that could signal a changed direction in the market place that warrants board attention. Benton is a contrary thinker; he believes that a board should have specialists for managing in boom times and entrepreneurs during recessions. The board will then receive the appropriate stimulus.

Leslie Thomas, Deputy Chairman of Caspen Oil PLC, chairman and independent director of several engineering companies

Thomas started his career as a naval constructor during the war before working in industry. He was at the time a production manager of Chubb before becoming an executive director. He later became managing director of a public company in the engineering sector. He has served on many engineering companies as an independent director and chairman.

The board's role

If one calls the outside directors independent then it follows that the executive directors should be classed as dependent. A seat on the board is often a reward for long-serving managers. The worst possible case for atrophy is a board loaded with senior dependent directors.

Ideally, a board should consist of an outside chairman, a chief executive, a finance director and independent directors. The best independent directors must be truly independent and have sources of income other than one particular set of fees. It is also desirable that they should be shareholders, having a further interest in the company's prosperity along with the other shareholders.

A chairman should foremost understand the company's business. For example, a company in the rubbish collection business dealing with a number of independent operators may not be in waste disposal, more likely they are in the prime contractor business.

- The first question to the board is, what business are we in?
- The second is what business should we be in?

Many boards are absorbed with the minutiae of operating statements and capital expenditure because they have lost the capacity to think about these issues.

The chairman's role

The chairman has a very different role from the managing director. The former is there to see that the board as a whole devises the strategy of the business; the chief executive is there to implement the tactical aspect of policy by making the best use of assets.

The next essential consideration is to have a finance director who is directly responsible to the board for providing a true and fair view of the business – an adviser to the board. This may place the finance director in something of a dilemma. On the one hand he owes a loyalty to the board as a whole, on the other he is subordinate to the chief executive.

Those around the board table should be aware of their potential contribution to a strategic plan. Many processes work according to a sine wave and business is no exception. The cycle certainly applies to products and to people, and the trick is to ensure that the wave is continually renewed to develop new managers and new products, and to generate cash and other assets.

The board can get stuck in the cycle because a number of older executive directors may become more concerned about the funding of their pensions than taking the company forward. A wonderful example is the hierarchy of the communist party in the Soviet Union before the lurch to democracy; most were there because they could not adapt and were determined to extend their privileges into retirement.

Independent directors

The independent director is there to serve the board as a whole and should not compensate for executive deficiencies by becoming a consultant – thereby losing objectivity. For example, if a board possesses sales (but not marketing) skills, an independent director who notices the deficiency should not fill the gap himself, but should insist that the role was properly defined and filled. To complete the objectivity it is essential for independent directors to be in the majority around the board table.

Thomas believes the best source of independent directors is from the boards of other industrial companies. This works in two ways; it provides the director with a wider base, while also adding strength to the other board. If a chairman wants to recruit an independent director, he should write to the chairman of other companies asking if one of his executives could be released for the purpose.

Another role for an independent director is to monitor the performance of the chairman and chief executive and, if necessary, to replace them. The first requirement is to ascertain the powers of the board for removing directors; thus one task for an incoming chairman is to ensure that this facility exists, based on a unanimous board vote which is endorsable at the next AGM. This again emphasizes the need to have a majority of independent directors.

If the independent directors have difficulties in changing the entrenched positions around the board table, they should consider approaching the institutions having first weighed the likely impact on other interested parties such as shareholders, customers, employees and local community. Quite often the mode of change is as important as the change itself.

Ronald Clark, investor and independent director

Ron Clark is an unusual outside director in that he acts both as a venture capitalist and a director in an investment. He is an engineer and became a venture capitalist almost by default. He had spent 25 years in GEC and Plessey and in the course of his service had accumulated capital through stock options (in those days a capital gain was taxed as income but could be rolled over if a trading asset was bought in lieu). In short, he persuaded the chairman to sell him several small businesses, among them Plessey Resistors and the intellectual copyright of a product in which he had previously tried to interest Plessey.

The companies prospered and some while later, Clark sold his largest company to BICC, joining the board at the same time. At about the same time British and Commonwealth bought the second largest company and quite recently he sold the last business. He describes the fascinating experience of being initially part of a big organization, then owning his own companies and then joining the board of a large industrial business. He is now relatively financially independent and is in the position of only dealing with situations which interest him.

Adviser to a venture capital company

Clark is now an adviser to Alan Patricof Associates Ltd (APA) and spends a significant proportion of his time exploring new situations or putting right those that have gone wrong; he also has the right to invest alongside APA. If the company is a start-up, Clark will evaluate the technology and people alongside the APA analysts. If one of the APA companies is going wrong he will assess the business and report back any requirements for remedial action or new capital. In both cases he is thoroughly familiar with all aspects of the company.

Ron Clark is now chairman of Radstone Technology PLC, a company which he had originally started while with Plessey, and in which he has a stake. Clark's involvement in Radstone was relatively straightforward for him; he knew the technology, the people and the business.

One remedial programme was Tetral, a hi-tech company in which APA had a 60% stake, with the executives owning 40%. The business was losing money, the board was in disarray and the company was out of control. Clark thoroughly analysed the business giving the company itself a clear trading bill of health, but the management needed control; new capital was needed and Clark became both chairman and a shareholder. He is also involved with APA in other hi-tech companies.

Problems dealing with venture capital supported companies

Clark believes that much could be done by venture capitalists to improve company liaison, particularly in syndicated investments.

However, the biggest investors of all are the banks. All is plain sailing when the companies proceed according to plan, but cracks appear when the business starts losing money, then the several parties can lose orientation.

Unlike the large investing institutions, venture capitalists and associated banks do not have a way of coordinating their activities. For example, some banks may want to put in investigating accountants, others may seek immediate receivership; some investors want to pull out, while others may be prepared to invest further. This means that a chairman of a syndicated investment often has considerable difficulties in getting decisions between the parties, particularly if remedial action or new money is needed.

The confused situation is made even more complex by companies like 3i changing their investment controllers or the banks their local managers. Clark strongly recommends that any chairman of a company owned jointly by venture capitalists and banks should make quarterly contact reporting to all such parties. This has three major benefits:

1 The individuals responsible for the investment are required to take notice.
2 They are informed of the position.
3 They have time to formulate a response if one is needed.

Clark recommends that where possible, a company requiring venture capitalist support is well advised to seek the smallest number of investors – even accepting a worse financial deal.

Independent directors tend to fall into two categories. First, there are the senior executives who are invited to sit on the boards of other companies in mid-career to widen their experience. Then there are those who take early retirement, and take one or two directorships to supplement their pension. This is fatal because if an individual cannot afford to lose fees then it will not be in his interests to speak out when he should; he may also fail to make the proper enquiries before joining a board, which can place him in a potentially embarrassing situation.

In Ron Clark's view, a potential independent director should want to join a board because he has a genuine interest in the business and the contribution they can make if he or she is appointed to represent the venture capitalist then the institutions should take the individual completely into their confidence and give him every backing.

Rob Johnson, lecturer at the London Business School on entrepreneurship

Rob Johnson is himself a successful American entrepreneur who, having sold his business, was rewarded with a case-study write-up by the Harvard Business School. He and his family now live in London.

Johnson is a firm believer in independent directors, having used them to advantage in his own affairs. Outsiders are needed to monitor an executive management team and should have experience from the industry or from suppliers or customers; there should also be someone with financial experience. The board should keep closely in touch with the shareholders, their aims and aspirations.

Finally one of the team needs to have a close rapport with the entrepreneur. Unlike a large company with many managers, entrepreneurs can feel very lonely; they need someone they can trust – an individual prepared to spend time perhaps mulling over some critical problems.

Supporting the entrepreneur

Entrepreneurship is leadership in a business situation where an individual is driven by the passion, desires, goals and imagination to succeed and is able to transmit this vision to others. Size is not as critical as skill and aptitude. Assessing the skills of the entrepreneur is probably the most important task of an outside director, the next critical question is whether the leader realizes his own strengths and weaknesses.

An experienced businessman acting as an outside director should be able to identify the early warning signs of an entrepreneur moving beyond his competence. For example, he needs to decide whether the individual can expand beyond the initial organization, institute appropriate controls and procedures and delegate to hired professionals. Some people can take the business forward to a large listed enterprise, like Alan Sugar of Amstrad, while others cannot.

Helping an entrepreneur is not easy, some have the confidence and wisdom to accept an outsider, others find it difficult to believe that another can know enough about the business to make a contribution. Most venture capitalists understand the problem and say they would rather invest in good people and a mediocre idea than a terrific idea and mediocre people. They reason that good people are smart enough to recognize their own limitations; if the critical point was reached, they would bring in someone to help. If the venture capitalists do not insist that an outsider be appointed they may be faced later with the choice of firing the chief executive or attempting to pull out their capital.

Outside director qualifications

It would be helpful if the incoming director had knowledge of the industry; it saves time and avoids long explanations by the chief executive. Basically, Johnson believes that outside directors should initially keep to their areas of expertise, finance, marketing, technical etc; when they join the board, they can make their enquiries and can then add to discussions quite quickly. From there they can move on to other areas and broaden their contribution.

The board should also understand the three or four critical items that make the difference between success and failure. This minimizes the need for directors to wait for problems to show up in the operating statement, they can be identified in advance. For some companies, for example, these might be the sales conversions on quotations, for others it might be the inventory held by distributors.

Whatever the business, the directors should be aware of the old saying that 'by the time problems hit the financial statements, they are way beyond correction'. The only way to prevent this problem is to understand what underlies the assumptions.

It is essential that an independent director forms a view on the strengths and weaknesses of the individual running the business – to correct an imbalance if possible. For example, a highly motivated and skilful marketing man could need the support of a good control system, not additional scrutiny of the sales plan. If the chief executive is an accountant or engineer then the independent director might be a marketing specialist. The independent director's first task should be to look for the balance that creates a whole rounded business.

Another task for the independent director is to determine the best time for the shareholders to harvest their investment. Most venture capitalists are quite prepared to watch their capital grow as the business expands and to put in more money if the company is still capable of growth. Others may see a limitation and sell the business to others who could do a better job.

Garry Lefevre, independent director

Garry Lefevre started his career with Price Waterhouse who sent him abroad to Switzerland, then Austria. He moved to join Morgan

Guaranty Trust as their controller for Belgium and Holland which led him back to the UK and treasurer of the Nationwide Building Society before it merged with the Anglia.

Lefevre was then out of a job but with a leaving package was able to go out on his own as a boardroom consultant, particularly strategic planning. He believes directors should plan at least one year ahead, where the company is going, how it is going to get there and what means they have to monitor their progress to the goal. Another role for a director is to act as a consultant; for example, Lefevre has prepared a stock option plan for executives of an international group.

Lefevre cites an example of a venture capitalist backed business which had reached sales of £3m over 10 years and had little idea what to do next. Creating a forward strategy needed substantial time with the principal in order to understand the business, before considering and arriving at a way ahead. To show the complexity of the problem, Lefevre reported that the chief executive's view changed completely from the start of the meeting to the end.

Another assignment was a large firm of architects who had a financial crisis and called in Lefevre to assist. After working on the crisis, he moved on to evaluate the architects, not as professionals but for their commercial skills. The practice has now been retained for substantial projects on the Continent and Gary is non-executive chairman.

David Darke industrial adviser and independent director

David Darke joined Taylor Woodrow as a graduate trainee then gained a wide experience in the construction industry during the 1970s before becoming managing director of Alexander Sutherland on behalf of the Bank of Scotland. Darke became an industrial adviser to 3i in 1981 and has since been involved with construction industry related companies like Phoenix Timber with the backing of 3i.

Dealing with disasters

In the construction industry, failure is most frequently the result of inability to read the market, or poor financial controls; it seldom arises from technical shortcomings. Mostly it is a failure through doing too well. Many companies overtrade, they try to expand on too small a financial base. In the construction business it is quite possible to run a £2m turnover on a capital of £50,000.

Syndicated loans in a buy-out and other multi-bank operations

Darke reports considerable difficulty dealing with the squabbles of clearing banks reconciling their collateral charges over a company's assets. He reports spending as much time resolving the banks' differences as running the business. He found a similar problem dealing with syndicated venture capitalists particularly when things started to go wrong. Support came from the houses that had both loans and investments while some with only investments wanted to pull out. With any luck, investors can be taken out if the business is bought by a larger group.

Briefing before entering a venture capital situation

As Ron Clark found, the most satisfactory company introduction is for the prospective independent director to be part of the investment investigation; to be briefed just before entering a venture capital investee company may not be all that helpful. All depends on how much the investment executive actually knows and can pass on. A new independent director should do a considerable amount of homework before entering an unfamiliar situation. Contact with the auditor of a construction company may not always be very satisfactory – most experienced directors can hide almost what they like in the work in progress.

The role of an independent director

Darke feels that an independent director should not speak for any particular investor, he should be responsible for the board as a whole; however, a letter of appointment should include the right for a two-way relationship with the sponsor. Most buy-out executives are technically competent but have little experience of independent operation; unfortunately some individuals cannot stand the new conditions and they have to leave. As a matter of principle, Darke likes to take a small stake in any company that he joins to show a commitment to the executives.

Supporting an entrepreneur

This is a very personal relationship as reported by Rob Johnson. Successful individuals are strong willed but with any luck, will consult the independent director before making a decision. To be successful, an independent director should gain the trust of the entrepreneur by quickly learning about the business, meeting the people and visiting the sites. Once the entrepreneur has confidence in the outsider, the independent director can expect to be used as an investigator – as a sort of 'second opinion'. Darke would encourage 'one man bands' to introduce general managers into the operating divisions in case anything happened at the centre.

Frank Ruhemann, independent director

Frank Ruhemann started his career in the early 1950s joining as a graduate engineer within the TI group. It was then almost an investment company with a series of unconnected businesses and he worked as an engineer in various subsidiaries before being appointed production manager in a machine tool company in Bedford in the late 1950s. He was there around 18 months when TI bought British Aluminium and new chairman, Lord Plowden, picked him as his PA.

Learning his trade in TI

Ruhemann was involved with helping to make TI into a modern international group by forming like subsidiaries into divisions and disposing of those businesses that did not fit. When the time came for him to move on he understudied the chairman of Aluminium Foils, a subsidiary of Reynolds Aluminium in the USA. Shortly after taking the appointment the chairman died and Ruhemann tackled the job of making the business profitable with only marginal help from the group. His methods are instructive:

- Instead of using costly consultants, Ruhemann asked individuals at many different levels to research and tell him about the markets, products and techniques, each in their own segment. This formed the basis of a new strategy with winnable opportunities.
- The company standardized the specification of milk bottle covers by experimenting with gauge and width variations. They also rationalized 50 shades of gold down to five which then became the industry standard. Any other colour could be supplied providing the customer paid the set-up charge.

After six years, Ruhemann started a company doctoring and strategic unit within TI, recruiting bright people within the group leavened with one or two MBAs. The team was much in demand concentrating on the core businesses and building up the automotive side. Eventually he was asked to deal with Raleigh Bicycles, which was then losing £18m a year and threatening the group's credibility. Ruhemann was given a free hand either to write it off, give it away, or turn it round – anything.

Turning around Raleigh

Raleigh had been the graveyard of many reputations and as he walked around the 62-acre site, he wondered if the company would claim him as well. His plan of action was as follows:

- The directors first option was closure and they set out a plan which would have cost £40m to implement. Secondly they considered a sale to one of the market leaders which included Merida in Taiwan, another in Japan, Huffey in Chicago and two profitable TI plants in Canada and Holland.
- It was agreed that any action should be calibrated against world-class players and a TI task force was set up to make a survey led by a McKinsey consultant. The results were fascinating. The best companies took 60 minutes to assemble a bicycle, Raleigh took 140. The overheads per 100,000 bikes ranged from nine people in Chicago to 54 in Nottingham. Finally, the lead time for the Taiwanese was 3/4 days, in Nottingham no one really knew.
- It was decided to put individuals in charge of analysing the main modules such as tubing, welding, spokes etc and to determine how to manufacture a batch of 500 bicycles using Japanese quality circle techniques. The unions recognized the problem and co-operated by halving the workforce.
- Eventually the same number of bicycles was produced from a third of the space with a lead time of 10 days and the balance of the factory and the machinery sold. Luckily there was no problem with demand, the salesmen could sell everything they made.
- Ultimately, Raleigh was sold as a buy-out under a programme of concentration masterminded by Chris Lewington, the next chairman.

An independent director

Ruhemann retired from the TI board when he reached 60 and is now on the board of Powell Duffryn, Condor, and F L Schmitt, the

Danish conglomerate's UK arm called Anglo Nordic. He believes that the main contribution of an outside director should be to:

- Help with company strategy. Ruhemann believes that strategy should be considered in a global context. The questions should be asked, who are the best, what makes them so good, have they blind spots and then, what can be done? It is critical to decide how any business can be raised to the highest standard within a given market. It is something the Japanese are particularly good at.
- Question the strategy – particularly a diversification or an acquisition. He recommends that before any action is considered, the board should start with a clean sheet of paper, consider the options, then progressively home in on the alternatives that should be considered in detail.
- Improve the quality of the board's work, if necessary by replacing the chief executive or chairman. He believes it is important to analyse in detail what happens when a company makes a strategic mistake such as an acquisition that has signally failed to perform. The outside directors are at their most potent when they can work together.

15

Views of experienced chairmen

What the chairmen do and think

This chapter reports on how some of the top chairmen in Britain's larger companies see their job, how they run their board and what they expect from their independent directors.

These are the key points made by individuals working in very different kinds of mainly larger businesses. The authors are grateful for time given by extremely busy men.

The chairman's job

- The primary role of the chairman is to see that the board has the correct strategy for managing the resources of the business on behalf of the shareholders.
- One of the chairman's primary jobs is to keep the correct balance in the agenda between strategic, tactical and monitoring issues.
- Many employees of a large company are encouraged if the

chairman is seen talking about their company or industry on TV or is written about in the press.

- Management by walking about and encouraging all management levels should take up a significant proportion of a chairman's time. For example, John Sainsbury would know when even a bag of sugar was out of place.
- A new chairman of a major company can expect to occupy at least 50% of his time learning the business, visiting as many sites as possible at home and abroad and meeting people.

External relations

- The broad targets should be communicated regularly to those most closely associated with the business such as the major shareholders and usually the lead bankers.
- Proposals that institutions should assume much of the corporate governance role undertaken by those in Germany and Japan, fail to take into account the system differences.
- An independent director ultimately has only one real weapon – resignation.

Working of the board

- A board's effectiveness is judged by its capacity to create, then implement board decisions. There is a distinct difference between the role of the chairman and chief operating officer – although these can be combined.
- A board's efficiency stems from its ability to make intelligent use of committees and from adequate board propositions and reports.
- Executive proposals to the board should not necessarily be presented as 'cut and dried' recommendations. It is for the board as a whole to reach a decision after due debate.
- A board should be balanced to reflect the needs of the business and the personalities around the board table. Some would argue that the composition should also change to meet economic circumstances; a three-year contract for independent directors is helpful in leavening the board to meet changes. Some companies also stick to a firm retirement policy for all directors.

Independent directors

- Not many people become independent directors in large companies for the money, most are there because of interest in the company and the contact around the board table. Their ultimate weapon is one they hope never to use – their resignation and its impact on major shareholders.
- 'Independent directors are very important to us, we communicate regularly with them and they make an enormous contribution'.
- An external monitor is essential if the executives have not lived up to expectations and changes have to be made.
- There is a potentially severe limitation to the number of senior executives prepared to serve either as a part-time chairman or independent director on other boards. This could be alleviated by mutual exchange.

Board's role in creating strategy

- Strategic lead times vary. For a large retailer, these largely revolve around purchasing land and erecting stores. Acquisitive conglomerates in contrast, often work on a different time scale and need a different type of person.
- 'Inspiration does not come from the USA – where store economics are quite different from the UK – but from market research. Grocery buying is known as the "drudgery shop" and we adapt our policy continually to the market weather vane.'

Summary of qualities required by a chairman

Strong basic convictions: one of the qualities listed by Hugh Parker as essential to creating the right ethos throughout the organization. For example, Sir Ian MacLaurin stresses total commitment to setting the highest standards of every aspect affirming the Tesco brand name.

Intellect: Parker states that it is not possible to run an organization of any size successfully unless this is driven by an intellect of high calibre.

Clear strategic vision is amply demonstrated by those who have radically changed their organization to meet changing needs.

Management experience seems to come in three variants. There is the professional who has successfully risen through many layers of management within a large organization and thoroughly understands the business. Others have skills which have grown with time in several organizations. Yet others have gained their skills by being involved in a wide variety of businesses; one key skill lies in picking up a brief quickly.

Political skills are implicit in the work of all those interviewed but they manifest themselves not so much in parliamentary terms but in eloquence. It is almost impossible to be a successful chairman of a large organization without the ability to speak about the business either face to face or to large groups of people – if necessary without notes or a prepared speech.

Mental energy: to have all the above qualities is one thing, but to have the curiosity and mental drive to put these into perspective is a singular quality given to few people.

Integrity: rising to the top of a large organization requires great ability, application and integrity. It also requires humility – a trait not normally found in powerful men. Where the role of chairman and chief executive are combined one or more independent directors are often included to monitor the top man's performance and tell him when it is time to go.

Flexibility becomes essential when dealing with uncertain market conditions and very rapid change.

This is what chairmen expect from their outside directors.

An external view

- An independent director should be able to present an outside view of the business to the executives.
- Significant contributions can be made from people who are outside the business. In particular some people have a particular gift for reporting on the way people think within an organization. A civil servant on secondment taught the board about Whitehall and learned about commerce. Where appropriate, an MP can inform the board about legislation passing through parliament.

Qualities

- Personalities are significant. Some will be questioning, others are there to support the executives, others may have valuable views which nevertheless need prising out of the individual.
- It is important to have a streetwise feel at the board table, both to encourage opportunities and warn of downside risks.
- There is no way that the chairman alone can have the range of experience necessary to create a strategy for a big organization. He needs independent directors and outside advisers to complement his skills.
- A national from another country is useful for learning about the business culture, it is generally not a good idea to ask for contacts or business advice.
- Fixed term contracts for the chairman and independent directors are an important method of rotating skills.

Individual chairmen

Below is a summary of meetings with individual chairman.

Sir Adrian Cadbury, Chairman Pro Ned, ex-Chairman Cadbury Schweppes

The board's job and the director's role

A well-constructed board should comprise a balance of skills and personalities which can vary with the economic circumstances. Unfortunately it may not always be possible to have the right people in place at the right time, although fixed terms of three years are helpful in re-arranging the pack. These are some of the considerations:

- There should be a balance between an inside view of the company provided by the executives and an external view provided by the independent directors.
- Changes in economic climate should be anticipated by the board. Quite often an outside director can see potential risks and opportunities more quickly than the executives.

- Although specialist skills are important, independent directors are there for their contribution to the board as a whole. To be most useful, they should be sufficiently well briefed to participate in strategic decisions and monitoring performance.
- The time horizon should be appropriate to the business; for example a heavy commitment to development would require a different set of people from, say, an acquisitive conglomerate.
- A national from another country can widen a board's perspective.
- A board member should not be recruited as a cheap way of gaining contacts or consultancy. There are professionals in both areas.
- Personalities should be balanced between those who challenge and those who are basically supportive.

The changing board

The primary role of the chairman is to ask the question: what sort of a company is it and in what time scale does it operate? Consequently, what kind of a board do we need?

- The board composition needs reshaping from time to time to meet changes in the business situation. There is some continuous change as individuals come up to retirement age or have completed their stint. This emphasizes the advantage of fixed contracts for the chairman and independent directors.
- Fixed term contracts have several advantages. At the end of a (say) three-year term a chairman can review with an independent director how the appointment is working. This works both ways. The chairman can reflect on the individual contribution and the independent director can respond with ideas on how the board can be more effective. A fixed term makes it so much easier to call it a day.

Monitoring performance

It is also important for a board to have a senior independent director, possibly the deputy chairman, who is regarded around the board table a powerful independent 'wise old bird'. His job is to monitor the chairman and, if necessary, tell him when it is time to go. The task is made more complicated, but more essential, if the role of chairman and chief executive are combined.

The board should pace itself by setting performance targets and measuring its own competence. Once these objectives have been agreed, they should be passed to important groups such as the major shareholders (without making them insiders) and banks. This is a useful marker for the board as a whole but the executives in particular. An outside appraisal is particularly important if executive changes have been made, such as after a disaster.

- Independent directors have an important role in setting markers for pacing the performance of the chairman and executives. By and large their monitoring role has not been a success in the early 1990s, but it is essential if changes have to be made for a declining performance without sound explanations.
- The institutions have a role to play in monitoring the board's composition and performance. In 1984, Cadbury Schweppes set out market share and financial targets to senior people among major shareholders as a means to pace the board. Fund managers were informed that they had the right to approach the chairman and voice dissatisfaction if the board were failing to meet agreed targets.
- Sir Adrian instances a suggestion by Martin Lipton that a board should be given five years to meet a stated objective; if they have not performed they should go and another group be appointed. This may be too precise a view but it establishes a written benchmark by which to judge the board as a whole and the chief executive in particular.

Removing the chief executive or chairman

The independent directors are usually the first to express dissatisfaction around the board table with the chairman or executives. Cadbury believes it important that this should be done openly.

- The first step is for one or more independent directors to approach the chairman to state their views. If their fears are put to rest, then all well and good.
- If the independent directors are not satisfied the criticism should be expressed openly around the board table with the independent directors reserving the right to approach the major shareholders (or the banks if appropriate).
- After an open conflict it is almost certain that one or the other parties will have to leave.

Banking relationships

The banks do not play the same corporate governance role as in Germany where they are also major shareholders. Syndicated loans have made banking relationships more complicated because there is not one single bank taking a long-term interest.

Banks only become involved in corporate governance in Britain if covenants have been broken and the lenders want their money out. Then they can require a number of conditions such as management or policy changes as a condition for further support.

Peter Davis, Chairman and Chief Executive of Reed International

Peter Davis went straight into business from school as a management trainee in an engineering company. After six years, he was attracted to marketing and joined General Foods which gave him experience in product management. The retail trade was becoming interested in marketing and he applied to Key Markets where he became marketing then managing director. Davis later joined Sainsbury as non-food director, then later assistant managing director in 1979.

Combining the role of chairman and chief executive

Davis joined Reed in 1986 as deputy chief executive just after Sir Alex Jarrett had retired and the then chief executive Les Carpenter had also become chairman. The decision whether the role of chairman and chief executive should be combined critically depends upon the individual.

Some chief executives are excellent at running a business but find it difficult to make the transition to a much more strategic and visible role. Others can contribute to both which is why many boards have accepted the dual role. Davis takes the view, echoed by many others, that large companies should have enough independent directors to remove the top person if this is the general will.

Unfortunately, many senior people in Britain, unlike the USA, believe that the next stage for a chief executive is to become a chairman for reasons of status, social standing etc. The transition is seldom successful because the two roles are different. One of the few people who have bridged the gap is Sir Adrian Cadbury who has filled both roles with distinction, partly because he knew the business well.

Style in a publishing group

A publishing group employs a number of creative people who often find difficulty giving of their best in a normal corporate structure. Davis found that he could adapt the visible leadership of walking around a retail store to that of a publishing company where he meets most people at their place of work. This individual contact requiring very personal leadership skills is often quite different from that usually found in manufacturing. The style pays off. After a short time in the job, Peter Davis found that he knew the names of 120 people attending an internal presentation of the annual results.

Apart from a visible role to the institutions and the media, Peter Davis places a high priority on strategy. In the case of Reed, this meant the final unwinding of Lord Ryder's 13 divisions to that of a pure publishing company.

The effective board

An effective board reflects a balance between strong executives who know the business and the outside directors. Both are necessary. Although answerable to the chief executive, executive directors should be able to take a strong line around the board table, knowing that their position is protected by contracts. In Davis's view, many of the failures in the early 1990s could have been avoided if strong executive directors (not independent directors) had acted as the brake on an adventurous chairman.

Reed has the normal Remuneration and Audit Committees staffed by independent directors – the chairman and finance directors sitting on the latter as ex-officio members. The compensation committee also has the job of monitoring executive performance and reporting to the chief executive if any one director is performing poorly. It would be only in extreme circumstances that the independent directors should seek to remove one of their executive colleagues.

The board meets eight or nine times a year. Apart from monitoring progress the executives are encouraged to bring plans to the board after the matter had been researched but not concluded – a fine distinction. This then gives the board the final say in matters of policy. The overriding test is whether the board as a whole (not just the executives) makes the correct decisions.

The independent director

The time that a company executive can spend working as an independent director may be unacceptable to the parent company, particularly if expenses are involved. There have been instances where independent directors could not have done their duty unless they were supported either by their parent company or by institutions. In one case an individual spent £150,000 of his own money on professional advice to fulfil his duty.

The increasing time demanded by executives acting as independent directors places a severe limitation on the potential pool of available individuals. Executives acting as independent directors or part-time chairmen should still retain their 'power base' to retain the urgency of decision making and their support if they are required to take difficult (and sometimes costly) decisions.

Jon Foulds, Chairman of the Halifax Building Society

Jon Foulds spends around 50% of his time as chairman of the Halifax, his other interest include 3i (where he was chief executive), Eurotunnel, Brammer, one or two investment trusts and Mercury Asset Management.

Summary of discussion

- There is really no such thing as a non-executive chairman. There can be times when the chairman has to use executive authority. Part-time chairman is a more accurate expression.
- The chairman oversees the development of strategy and the timing and manner of the presentation to the board of management's recommendations. He has to ensure the necessary balance of skills and outside experience is available round the board table to provide proper guidance.
- The appropriate composition of the board will vary according to the size of a business, its nature, and the particular stage in its development.
- The chairman has a particular responsibility for the external influences bearing on a business. He should therefore know, ideally at first hand, his way around Whitehall and Westminster.
- The Halifax has over 20,000 employees. Board members need to know the problems of running such a large organization, and to understand both the opportunities and the drawbacks of size.

- The Halifax is a retailer of financial services. The input of a director drawn from a major stores group could be particularly useful in ensuring sensitivity to the marketplace, and the problems of running 730 branches.
- The Halifax needs specialist skills on Board Committees. Among these is the Treasury Committee, which is concerned with the risk profile of the balance sheet and the use of sophisticated derivative instruments.
- In a financial organization, the Audit Committee has a particularly onerous task. It should be chaired by a non-executive director with appropriate skills.
- Above all, the Board should have a collective wisdom arising from personal qualities and the balance of skills to apply to opportunities or set-backs as they arise.
- The Halifax has a Chairman's Committee which includes all members of the chair and one other non-executive director. It meets monthly to discuss the course of current business and to pre-digest informally some of the more difficult issues. It would not work as well as it does if the board, as a whole, saw it as an inner cabal.
- All good boards need at least two non-executive directors to act in concert when necessary, for example to invite the chairman to retire. Their ultimate joint sanction of resignation could send appropriate signals to shareholders, regulators and others.
- The chairman is responsible for the board agenda and the timely presentation of both tactical and strategic issues. He is also responsible for the correct balance of board discussion recorded in the minutes.
- Independent directors should be appointed for a definite period (of say six years) which gives the chairman an opportunity progressively to change the board composition in line with the changing needs of the business.
- Board building is a minor art and one of the tests of a good chairman. Another is the selection of his successor.

Sir John Harvey-Jones, Deputy Chairman of Grand Metropolitan (Author of *Making It Happen*, *Getting it Together* and other books)

As chairman of ICI, Sir John's prime task was to manage the board itself. This involved not only setting and managing the work programme, but also selecting, coaching, rewarding and (sometimes) punishing his colleagues. The board's time is very expensive and needs a high level of management skills to generate the added value required from each level in the organization.

The management style created by the top board creates a 'pyramid' of behaviour that should be reflected at all levels in the organization. If the chairman projects a consistent image then this will be projected both directly through the company and via the media.

These are some of the issues raised by Harvey-Jones which should be read in conjunction with his most readable book *Making it Happen*.

- The chairman of ICI is selected by secret ballot of the directors with the votes counted independently. This means that the leader has a consensus around the board table where he is only *primus inter pares*. Sir John required that his mandate be reviewed three years into his five years as chairman.
- As chairman he took great care in projecting the agenda for future board meetings. This was to ensure that the board discussed the most significant issues facing the company at the right time. The pattern was set up after considerable consultation with other board members and implied a rolling forward demand on the staff to prepare the necessary papers and research well in advance.
- There can be only one individual who can project the company to the outside world. In some companies it might be a powerful chief executive, in the majority of companies it should be the chairman.
- It is exceptionally important that all the relevant voices are heard before a decision is made. It is up to the chairman to create the physical and personal setting for the various interactions around the board table to reach the best conclusion. Harvey-Jones worked through formal and informal meetings to ensure the best possible discussion took place.
- The prime responsibility of the board is to generate a strategy on the time scale appropriate for the business. In breaking down the policy for each division it is essential to give the maximum headroom for individuals to display flair and initiative.
- The board should also see that the appropriate organization is in place to implement the strategy and to ensure that there is a valid training and succession policy.
- The chairman has the opportunity to stamp his own ideas on the board and to ensure the composition reflects the needs of the business. There was parity between executive and independent directors at ICI and Sir John made considerable changes. These included recruiting German and Japanese nationals to give the company a direct understanding of operating in these countries.

- If a company is in a vicious spiral of decline when things are going wrong, it is essential for the chairman to take the initiative to reverse the trend.

Independent directors are essential to balance the skills around the board table and where possible there should be a continuous opportunity for changing the composition. These are some of the important ingredients:

- It is helpful for someone to understand the City and to act as a counterpart to the financial director.
- Depending upon the business there should be someone with the relevant technology skills likely to be found from academe.
- Personalities are important, a balance between thinkers and action men, extroverts and introverts.
- It is helpful to have foreign nationals to give the board a cultural insight to the main markets.
- Independent directors have a particular role in monitoring the executives. Sir John is Deputy Chairman of Grand Metropolitan and leads a special group of independent directors three or four times a year in separate meetings. This is done with the full agreement of their executive colleagues.

Sir Ian MacLaurin, Chairman of Tesco PLC

The Tesco founders did an outstanding job creating a retailing business that was a national leader during the 1950s and 1960s. The company declined somewhat in the 1970s because the founders' family were content with their success and were enjoying the wealth it brought to them.

This was not a satisfactory situation for Ian MacLaurin (who had been recruited by the president in 1959) and other executives who had joined the company as management trainees and were then at board level. At one board meeting in 1976 he and his colleagues successfully challenged the founder family members (with the help of an outside director) and set about re-positioning the company.

It began with the decision to pull out of Green Shield Trading Stamps and to pass the benefit of keener prices on to customers. This was a success which heralded other cultural changes introduced by professionals who had come up through the business.

The strategy

Sir Ian's main contribution was to have a very clear vision where he wanted the business to go. The work was driven by his insistence that everything should be of the highest quality. This applied to own label brands, store layout, engineering standards, quality of architecture – everything.

These standards are inviolable and it took him and his team five years to get the business into shape before the results started to come through. MacLaurin pays tribute to the superb team around him which were present in 1976. Almost all are still there.

The results have been remarkable. In 1982 the company made a profit of £43m which grew to £417m in 1991.

Tesco's strategy is governed by the lead time to open new stores. Each one costs about £25m and takes five years from planning application to opening, which demands a rolling three-year pro-gramme. The inspiration for the new look at Tesco stems not from American experience (where the economics are quite different) but from internal and external market research.

The public perception of buying groceries is known as the 'drudgery shop'. The principles remain the same but the practice changes over time and plays a powerful part in creating group strategy. Apart from regular policy meetings, each year the board meets away from the office at Brocket Hall, near Hatfield, for two days to discuss strategic issues.

Sir Ian's vision of the enterprise continues to be UK retail based. This is the business he and his team know and understand and there is no creative incentive to go down the same route as Asda, Next and Burton. The main task before them is to steer the company through the 1990s as there is much to do in Britain while still keeping overseas contacts, particularly in Europe and the USA.

MacLaurin insists on regular communication with shareholders. Either he, his managing director or finance director visits the main institutions on a regular basis to discuss with them the aims and objectives of the group.

The independent directors

Tesco has four non-executive directors and one part-time executive director, Victor Benjamin, who also serves as deputy chairman and sits on the remuneration and audit committees. All bring to the board a wide range of expertise and are there to monitor the executives.

The others are John Padovan, deputy chairman of BZW, who chairs the audit committee, John Gardiner, the chairman and chief executive of the Laird Group, Baroness O'Cathain who is managing director of the Barbican Centre and Francis Krejsa, chairman of a subsidiary company Spen Hill Properties. Each makes a strong contribution. MacLaurin is particularly keen to promote women within the organization.

In a sense Tesco is more easy to manage than a multinational organization. They have nearly 400 stores in the UK, employ some 90,000 people and have annual sales of £6.5bn.

The Guinness involvement

Sir Ian with four others, was appointed to the board of Guinness by the Bank of England and Stock Exchange when the previous chairman reneged on the Distillers offer document commitment to make Sir Thomas Risk chairman. The team went on the board in the Autumn of 1986 and their monitoring work really started when the DTI inspectors came in during December.

After Ernest Saunders left in January 1987, Sir Norman (now Lord) MacFarlane became chairman and the independent directors effectively ran the group for six months, recruiting a new chairman – one of their number becoming chief executive. The institutions were totally behind the move.

Alan McLintock, Chairman of the Woolwich Building Society and other companies

Some while ago, Scottish accounting firms generally took a wide view of their profession by allowing partners to join their client's boards. There were some problems about conflicts of interest but 30 years ago it was not perceived to be an insuperable difficulty. The number of directorships were limited to two, more than this would detract from their auditing role. McLintock particularly became involved on the board of Unit Trusts and through them was asked to go on the board of Queen Anne's Hotels, the holding company for the Hyde Park Hotel, Quaglinos etc.

McLintock continued with Trust House when it acquired Queen Anne's but left after the merger with Forte. From then, further opportunities presented themselves such as the Woolwich Building Society and National Westminster Bank. Ten years ago there were no conflicts of interest between being on the advisory boards of banks and building societies. Today, it would be unusual (to say the least) to find a bank director on a building society board or vice versa. McLintock retired from the bank board in 1990. He had other involvements such as the M&G group and the Ecclesiastical Insurance Office.

McLintock holds the strong view that the chairman and chief executive should be different people. The roles are distinct and complementary – the possible exception being the big clearing banks, where chairmen have a major ambassadorial role.

The chairman's first task is strategic and to do this he must learn, and keep closely in touch, with the grass roots of the business. For example the Woolwich has some 550 branches, the powerhouse of the business at the end of the executive communication channels.

Some years ago, the chairman instituted a number of regional dinners where independent directors go around the country in pairs to meet groups of branch managers 12 to 15 at a time. After dinner there is a two-hour discussion, not to talk about administration but to learn about the business first hand.

This is a two-way discussion. The board hears from the 'sharp end' and tells the local managers something of the board's thinking.

As chairman of the Woolwich, McLintock sees independent directors as trustees and advisers to the organization. They must keep clear of day-to-day duties but are there to supervise the executives and ensure they are accountable, particularly at the strategic level. Strategic thinking can arrive at the board two ways; most often this arises from the executives but sometimes ideas originate from the independent directors. The ideas are then discussed around the board table and, when agreed, become Society policy.

The Woolwich occupies about a third to a half of McLintock's time. The main board meets regularly once a month but there are a number of committees. The board agenda is in two parts. The first receives and monitors divisional and committee reports, the second deals with specific topics for wider review.

Among the operating committees, the Woolwich have a bi-monthly chairman's committee made up of the chairman, deputy chairman and two or three of the independent directors. This group meets quarterly for discussion of important matters between board meetings and at least once a year, the full board has a two-day planning meeting to consider a rolling five-year programme and related strategic issues.

The independent directors have a very significant role in reporting matters as they see it from outside the business. This is particularly important in companies with large career structures like banks where the executives get little view from outside the company. To overcome this banks have regional advisory boards composed of local businessmen who make a useful input.

At the Woolwich, the board is made up of skills appropriate to the industry, although the exact division is not fixed. There are, for example, those with financial experience, then those close to the industry such as builders and surveyors. Legal and economic talents are also useful but all directors are expected to contribute as independent individuals, not exclusively as specialists.

Politicians can be useful in keeping the board abreast with parliamentary issues affecting the industry.

The role of independent directors varies between industry and the financial sector. In the latter, it has been the custom to have a large number of independent directors with only perhaps the chief executive on the board. This has now changed and boards in the financial sector include an increasing proportion of executive directors.

In financial institutions a ratio of 1:2 executives to independent directors is about right. In industry the ratio is probably the reverse, although the proportion is now growing. One independent director on his own can only make a limited contribution and there should be at least two. Whatever the number, independent directors should get to know the organization, be inquisitive and learn about the business and how it works.

First-class directors can come from other than the professions associated with the industry. For example, the Woolwich has two women on the board (until recently three) and they have a distinctive role in spheres like personnel matters. Another potential source is the civil service who are sometimes prepared to second promising members to outside boards for a limited period. The communication is two-way. Companies get a feel for the working of Whitehall and the civil servant benefits from exposure to commercial pressures. Other very useful contributions can be made by senior executives from industrial companies if they can be released to serve on other boards.

Hugh Parker, ex-Managing Director of McKinsey, London and Chairman of Corporate Renewal Associations Ltd

When the limited liability company was established in the eighteenth century, it created the possibility for ownership to be separated from management. It also made it possible for shareholders' investment to be limited, irrespective of the liabilities that the company would be required to meet. The bridge between the company and the shareholders is the board of directors; and the directors' overriding responsibility is to the shareholders.

The difference between a management meeting and a board meeting is the presence of independent directors who are not employees of the company. Their presence is there to ensure that the board reaches a 'critical mass' capable of evaluating, then implementing, a strategy. In Parker's view, a board without independent directors is not a board at all – their presence changes a management group into a board of directors.

The minimum number of independent directors should be three, if they are strong characters, but it is better that there should be parity with the executives. This is not for voting purposes but to achieve a consensus taking into account a number of varying views. If a board cannot agree on a difficult decision then it is better that the proposition be re-thought. Parker cites an occasion when board dissidents were told that they had better accept a decision or resign – and if they did not resign, be fired!

Irrespective of the intellect, commitment, wisdom or experience of the independent directors they are only as good as the chairman's ability to mobilize their talents.

In an article printed in *Long Range Planning* (see References), Hugh Parker states that successful chairmen tend to share five key qualities:

- They hold strong basic convictions about the kind of company they want to lead, its values and standards. They have a strong commitment to the future and believe in giving others the room and opportunity to excel. In Sir John Harvey-Jones' words 'creating tomorrow's company from today's'.
- A clear strategic vision stems from strong convictions and endows leaders with the ability to project a clear-cut message for the future understandable at all levels within the business and outside. Since the future, by definition, is only a set of probabilities it is essential that the chairman lays down clear goals, standards and priorities and provides the team with the resources for the achievement.
- Intellectual capacity is an essential attribute. It is not possible to be a successful chairman unless there is the highest capacity for rigorous analysis, logical reasoning, innovative thinking and for making rational decisions.
- He must have substantial management experience to know and understand how organizations should be structured and managed to make a profit. In Parker's view this can only be achieved by

working up through the various levels and it places chairmen without such experience at a disadvantage.

- Political skills are defined as the exercise of power within an organization using techniques such as persuasion, motivation, relationships, even threats, for obtaining agreement and compliance. Parker explains that Machiavelli's Prince was not evil or cynical, just a realist who understood that one aspect of leadership was the manipulation of people, otherwise known as politics.

Contrasting the USA and UK approaches to board composition

In the USA the Chairman is usually also the Chief Executive Officer and the President is the Chief Operating Officer. These are two quite distinct roles. The chairman is responsible for strategy and for shareholder liaison, the president is there to run the business. In addition, there will usually be a majority of outside directors around the board table.

Making a broad distinction, the chairman is there to project the company to the outside world and to reflect what is happening externally back into the business. In general, he is primarily concerned with the longer-term future of the company.

By contrast, the chief operating officer is primarily concerned with the affairs of today, getting it right now and keeping the organization tuned. This does not mean that the executives should be kept out of strategic issues, many of these ideas often come from within the company.

In Britain the pattern varies because, in a number of companies, the chairman is also the chief executive. There may be good reasons why the duties are combined but there can be conflicts of interest which have been pointed out by the prime shareholder body and Institutional Shareholder's Committee.

Historically, financial companies and banks have had a majority of independent directors around the board table while industrial companies have very few. Parker reports that the latter group are tending toward parity between executive and independent directors.

Finally, certain qualities are particularly important in the role of the independent director:

- Three qualities are essential: detachment by objectivity and independence. Without these, he will be of little value.
- Corporate finance skills are useful to most boards. These provide knowledge of how to raise short- or long-term loans, the treasury function and raising equity funds.

- A multinational firm like Unilever or Shell with a combined Anglo-Dutch board has enormously strong presence in its major operating areas and is not going to stumble because of being unaware of the risks in any part of the globe. If Parker were the chairman of a substantial company he would like someone from a company of this stature to be on his board.

- A board needs at least some streetwise individuals. This quality, which blends scepticism, realism, practicality, opportunism and common sense is often found in the board of an acquisitive company but may be lacking around a more conventional board table. If it is not present, it should be sought.

- Specific functional skills can be of particular value, depending on the company and circumstances. For example, technological understanding possibly from universities if the business is driven by certain techniques or principles not well understood by others around the board table: or marketing skills, when the company lacks a strong market presence.

- It is important that the individual can express himself succinctly, and focuses his contribution towards 'his own ground'. Board meeting time is limited and it does not help if every director insists on contributing irrespective of the subject.

- A good training ground might be the exchange of directors between companies of differing sizes. Main board or divisional directors of larger companies might go on the board of smaller companies as independent directors. There is a two-way benefit from this exchange.

Sir David Plastow, Chairman and Chief Executive of Vickers PLC

Sir David's most important responsibility is to see that Vickers has the right strategy in place and the right people to run it, on behalf of the shareholders. This requires highly focused personal disciplines to set the right priorities to those affected inside and outside the business.

Strategic responsibility is an ongoing commitment which includes spending at least two days a year off-site with senior colleagues. In the spring of each year, each division submits its forward proposals for discussion by the executive committee before being formally debated by the board. Unlike companies with a divided chairman and chief executive, Plastow occupies the central role of communicating the general board strategic plan to the divisions, then taking the lead in referring the completed plan back to the board as a whole.

Working through a strategic plan is particularly important for a multi-disciplined engineering company like Vickers. Over a 10-year period, the group has acquired or disposed of 50 operations in reaching its present shape. Sir David reckons that most subsidiaries have enough headroom to perform reasonably in the recession with the exception of the car division that has already reduced its break-even point. Recessions affect tactics rather than strategic issues, it means one has to be quicker on one's feet and keep a strong balance sheet.

Vickers have formal audit and remuneration committees which are led by the non-executive deputy chairman (while the role of chairman and chief executive are combined) and composed of independent directors. There is also the executive committee with the prime responsibility for creating strategy; this group is further strengthened by Professor John Stockton of the LBS who works with the director of corporate development. Vickers has a good spread of independent directors including engineers, those from the City and some with an entrepreneurial flair; each director is on a three-year contract and there is a retiring age of 65. Just recently a head-hunter was hired to recruit another independent director who was the managing director of a company the same size as Vickers.

Sir Peter Walters, Chairman of the Midland Bank

Sir Peter started his career at BP after graduating at Birmingham University with a degree in economics. He then did national service and recalls passing out as top cadet at Officer Cadet School. Believing he would be sent to an overseas posting of his choice he requested Singapore. It was not to be. A general's son took precedence although well down the list!

Walters was invited onto the board of BP at the age of 40 after serving in the planning department and two tours in the USA. He became chairman of the company at 50 where he was primarily responsible for strategy and running the main board consisting of five divisional managing directors and a majority of independent directors.

Sir Peter likens the group board of a large company to an army structure. As chairman he had the equivalent to Eisenhower's job during the Overlord operation. There was the central staff under his direct control and each army commander reported directly to him. Walters commiserates with the prime minister who has to use the Treasury as his staff headquarters; this is rather like Eisenhower having to rely on Montgomery's own staff for running several armies.

Combining the role of chairman and chief executive is not a real problem in a large company. These businesses all have a strong presence of independent directors to act as checks and balances. For example, at Thorn/EMI, Walters is deputy chairman where the other independent directors are Sir Graham Day, Sir Michael Angus, Professor Griffiths and David Barnes of ICI.

Sir Peter is also Chairman of Blue Circle which he joined after retiring from BP. He made a point of spending about 50% of his time for the first year just learning about the business, meeting the people, visiting the sites and learning how cement is made. He also decided upon a visible role with the press and media believing that it was important for the staff at all levels to see and read about their chairman before they met him in the flesh.

Walters is proposing a similar induction period at the Midland. Luckily the bank is now a fairly compact operation in the UK and Europe and he plans to spend half his time visiting branches and meeting people. Fortunately he does not have to spend too much time learning about the basic business because he was on the board of NatWest for a number of years.

Independent directors

It is important that at least half the independent director slots for larger companies be filled with individuals who still have a power base in industry or the professions. It is true that age brings wisdom but there is a certain loss of 'cutting edge' when individuals do not have to address the various executive decisions which are part of senior management. Finding the right people to become part-time chairmen and independent directors in the future is likely to create difficulties; the role is taking progressively more time and companies are becoming increasingly reluctant to cede the time of their top people to others.

16

Views of banks and insolvency practitioners

Independent directors do not usually see too much of their company's bankers, that is, until things start to go wrong. Then they should become very alert. If the board takes appropriate action, they should be able to save the company and preserve their reputation. If not, they could be in serious problems from the Insolvency Act.

Under the 1986 Insolvency Act independent directors may be deemed as culpable as the executive directors if their company is found to be guilty of fraudulent or wrongful trading. The definitions are laid down in Section 214 of the Act under which each director could be made to pay a personal contribution. This position has not been tested in the Courts, however, and there may be degrees of wrongdoing, for example if information for the board was deliberately withheld or distorted.

Bankers and insolvency practitioners who have to rectify board misjudgments seldom see directors at their best. In the spectacular failures of the early 1990s, it was shown that most independent directors did not understand their company's business and failed to control headstrong and entrepreneurial executives. This chapter aims to show what happens when a company exceeds its banking limits and covers:

- Understanding what is involved in a banking relationship and the trigger points that could make a bank take action to call in its loan.
- What happens when a bank calls in an investigating accountant.
- What alternatives the bank has available to remedy a deteriorating situation.
- What bankers have to say about non-executive directors.

In Britain, the clearing banks provide most of the loans to fund working capital for industry and commerce. The term of their loans tended to become longer in the 1970s and 1980s as the market for commercial paper declined. If a loan was required, a facility could be negotiated with one or more banks by the executive directors under a board mandate. In the vast majority of cases a good relationship would be built up based on trust between the bank and its customer. Many independent directors may not meet the bank manager, unless possibly after a board meeting over lunch. This is quite unlike shareholders whom independent directors will meet as a matter of course at annual general meetings.

Bank relationships usually remain harmonious until a stage in the economic cycle when interest rates rise and business declines – as occurred in the early 1990s (see Chapter 10). If the company is well managed the board will have anticipated the 'squeeze' between falling sales and fixed costs; if not, they could be in serious danger of running out of money, so forcing the bank to take action.

The people most to blame will be the executive directors but the independent directors also have a responsibility. The Insolvency Act shows no distinction between any members of the board when it comes to liability under fraudulent or wrongful trading. Their liability will, however, depend upon circumstances; in the worst case an independent director is deemed to be equally as responsible as the executives.

If the company's financial position deteriorates there will come a point when the bank will have a right to call in its loan. An investigation will follow and if the board is found culpable of creating credit (or continuing to lose assets) then the problems start. If directors are proved to have allowed their company to trade when they knew, or should have known, the business could not pay its bills then they may have to make a personal contribution to re-imburse the creditors.

Banking arrangements

Unlike shareholders whose relationship with the company is bound by company law, bankers are able to apply a range of conditions depending upon the risks of making an advance. For example, a bank making an advance to a jobbing builder might reasonably expect the loan to be repaid when a contract had been successfully completed and paid for. Quite different rules would apply to the competitive position of banks lending to, say, Hanson Trust or BP.

The rules for bank lending vary but most will have the following conditions:

- Loans are divided between those which are technically repayable within one year and those which are for a term, generally of some three or more years. Short-term loans will pay interest at a rate notified by the bank depending upon the size of the loan and the security of the borrower. Longer term loans may be at a fixed rate of interest.
- Banks like to review the conditions of each short-term loan (or 'advance') at the year end. If their customers are profitable, the review may be marked by a lunch at the local head office when there may be offers to use more of the bank's services. If the customer has been doing less well, it might even expect a reduction of the facility or tighter operating rules. Banks are very realistic; when a customer is doing well other banks will try to lend them money; when the going gets tough, the lending bank can afford to be much more strict.
- The facility letter will almost invariably include a set of conditions, or covenants, which if broken, give the bank the right to demand repayment. The covenants are generally tailor-made for each business – conditions applying to a manufacturer often being quite different to those for a retailer or a broker of financial services.
- Covenants vary with the business. A small company could have an overdraft limit secured on a specific asset; as the company grows, this might be secured by a floating charge on the fixed and current assets. For a management buy-out (which is unusually highly leveraged for the size of company) interest cover could be critical. In fact, most banks stipulate a gearing

covenant because 90% of failures occur through companies being poorly managed and/or over-borrowed.

- If the banks are in a strong enough position competitively, they can demand the right to specify the assets over which they have a charge. This means that if, in the last resort, the business is put into liquidation they have the right to repossession ahead of other creditors. Frequently lending will be secured by a floating charge over a group of assets which only 'crystallizes' in the circumstances defined in the documentation.
- Most banks require their customers to send regular monthly trading reports; similar to those submitted to board meetings. The statements may then be tested through a ratio analysis to check whether the company is nearing any of the limits.

Factors causing companies to break their covenants

They have borrowed too much for three main reasons:

1 Incompetence. The systems did not show a deteriorating position until it was too late.
2 Poor anticipation. Ably run businesses have key leading indicators to give early warning of a declining situation, poor managements do not. When problems reach the operating statement, it is usually too late.
3 Miscalculation. The board knows the position but believes that it can carry on as before because something good is about to happen. This might be the expectation of a large order or making a significant shipment. Usually, neither of these happens.

One of the most common causes of failure is to misjudge the business cycle (see Chapter 10). This means that boards find their company being squeezed by higher rates of interest just when their ability to pay higher charges is curtailed by falling sales. Typically the squeeze happens very suddenly, taking both bank and their customers by surprise. When investigators are sent in at the request of the bank to report on a company's affairs they almost invariably find that the situation is worse than was originally reported.

Failure rates vary with the business cycle.

- During the expansion phase few companies become endangered unless there is an unusual event such as a major contractual failure or even fraud.
- The crisis phase puts those companies at risk that have expanded too quickly on borrowed money, without realizing the risks involved. Sometimes firms can react quickly to repay debts or reduce costs, others fail to respond. The victims are generally in two categories:

  First there are the 'shooting stars' of former times whose management style strives for even greater expansion despite evident losses and cash shortages.

  Second there are smaller people in building and construction, retail, financial services, advertising, vehicle distribution etc whose market falls away when private spending falls.

- The liquidation phase is of the greatest danger because companies that survived the 'spike' in interest rates are caught by a steady decline in business which forces many to default. This is the time that the larger manufacturing companies are put under the greatest strain.
- The rate of failure will continue well after the bottom of the recession, and business activity will remain at a low ebb. However, the most successful companies that anticipated the working of the cycle will now be rich in cash and in a wonderful position to invest and expand.

Consequences of a company breaking its covenants

The banks differ in the way in which they monitor their customers. For example, Barclays and National Westminster run a central advances department which monitors the large accounts all over the world. If a customer looks like breaching a covenant, this account is then passed to an adjacent department specializing in intensive care. In the case of the Midland, advances are handled by the branch network and are only passed to the risk management department when the customers are seen to be in trouble.

The position is made more complicated when a number of banks is involved in a syndicated loan. In the mid-1970s and early 1980s, the Bank of England was involved on occasion in coordinating efforts to save troubled companies. In the late 1980s a memorandum was circulated, known as the 'London Approach', requesting all the bankers to a troubled company to work together in a rescue effort.

The initiative was not well received by all the parties – some foreign banks regarded the guidelines as an intrusion into their customer relationship. In almost every case a lead bank is appointed to manage the rescue; generally the one with the greatest exposure.

The banks' intensive care units are manned by skilled individuals whose prime task is to nurse customers back to financial health, if this is possible. These people, like insolvency practitioners and company doctors are above all, realists. They have a range of remedies at their disposal and genuinely feel a sense of failure if a business in their care has to be liquidated. Some of the departments are quite large – Barclays, for example employs some 60 people, mostly London based. If a company is of any size, the intensive care unit takes over the normal customer relationship once the covenants have been broken.

Their first task is to call in the senior management to understand the background and find out what the executives have done to stem the haemorrhage. If the measures are inadequate then the bank will impose a strict regime until a more permanent arrangement can be installed. At the early stage, a bank is likely to retain the present facility but may be forced in some cases to lend even more money. A customer in trouble will be expected to comply with the following:

- Trading out of problems is not a solution, increased sales only demand more working capital that cannot be funded.
- A rigid spending clamp-down on everything but urgent expenditure such as wages and the most outstanding creditors.
- Immediate first-aid measures to reduce unnecessary costs – whether these are fixed or variable.
- A central control over cash, cheque writing and movement of funds.
- Vigorous efforts to collect outstanding debts, unload excess inventory and sell luxury items such as yachts, racehorses or aeroplanes.
- Regular production of detailed cash-flow forecasts and reports.

How longer-term measures are initiated

Almost invariably, the bank will appoint an investigator (usually a specialist firm of accountants) to find out the true cash requirements of a business and recommend any long-term solutions. Although the lead bank may give instructions for the work, the company will always authorize the investigation and pay for the report.

Like intensive-care specialists, investigating accountants are a breed of their own who have spent many years building up expertise; many auditing accountants are just not suitable for the work. For example, Cork Gully (a major insolvency specialist) employed 800 people to cope with the recession of the early 1990s; they are a global concern with joint arrangements in Bermuda (specializing in insurance), South Africa, Ireland and the Far East.

The investigating accountants' brief will include a time scale depending upon the seriousness of the situation. If the bank senses that there is little hope of recovery they may need a quick confirmatory check before putting the business into liquidation; if there is likelihood of recovery, the enquiry may take several weeks. Whatever the duration, independent directors can ease the work of the investigators by encouraging the executives to cooperate. Investigators have to work fast and are expensive so it pays to have all the material at hand.

The main focus of an investigation will always be the balance sheet; a company will often have made losses before receiving the attention of the intensive-care unit – but it will invariably have run out of money. The investigators will concentrate on the following:

- Inventory including raw material and finished stocks and work-in-progress. Cork Gully have found that problems occur in optimistic valuations, poor recording and stock keeping, excessive profit taking and bad control of movement.
- Attention will have to be paid to the value of other potentially realizable assets such as investments, subsidiaries, property etc. The investigators will also be wary of asset values inflated through capitalizing interest.
- Receivables can often be overvalued because the company has unrealistic ideas on debt recovery. In one supposedly profitable company, the debtors had to be written down by almost one-

third because the directors had totally misjudged the debtors' inclination to pay.

- Directors of contracting companies can regulate their profits through contract valuation making it sometimes difficult for auditors to challenge the firm's valuation. In one business the profits were manipulated by working capital valuation which only came to light after acquisition. Then, much of the working capital was found to have a negative value!
- Balance sheets can be totally unrepresentative where large items of plant or aircraft are leased and their payment commitments and liabilities are hidden.
- Creditors may also not represent the true position due to poor book-keeping, either not disclosing the liabilities or delaying the entry.
- Where multi-national companies are involved the auditing problems are compounded because many countries do not have the same accounting standards found in Britain, the USA and in some European countries. The difficulties are made much worse if the executives are authorized to transfer large amounts of cash from one territory to another.

Actions following completion of the report

The investigators will keep closely in touch with the bank while the report is compiled as there may be times when exceptional action has to be taken to avoid further losses. On completion, the banks, the company management and the investigating accountants will meet to agree what happens next. In general, a report will include the following:

- A realistic balance sheet valuation and a report on the value of the bank's collateral.
- A report on the cash flow and the book-keeping systems.
- An assessment of the current budget and whether it will form a realistic starting point for a business plan; if not, the changes that are required.
- A comment on management quality.

The bank now has a number of options:

- The company may have responded to the crisis by the most likely combination of strengthening management, updating internal systems, selling surplus assets to reduce debt and reducing costs. Depending upon results the bank may be willing to make further advances and to convert short-term debt into a longer-term loan.
- The bank may give an ultimatum to the company to make the necessary changes or face the appointment of administrators or receivers. Often this may mean the board accepting a new director as a condition of continuing the facility.
- The creditors may petition the court to appoint administrators to run the business; although the bank or holder of a floating charge can override the petition, this no longer applies once the administrators have started work.
- Administration cancels the power of the directors; this is unlike the position in the USA where a moratorium under Chapter 11 allows the original management to run the business while creditors are 'frozen' at their previous levels. Under the Insolvency Act the administrators are there primarily to preserve the business as a going concern, wholly or in part; they should also conduct themselves on behalf of all the creditors for the most advantageous realization of the assets, compared to a liquidation.

The administrators will report the position to the creditors and may recommend a percentage debt reduction – what the Americans call taking a haircut. The company can now be passed back to the shareholders or the administrators can continue. During administration, the banks retain their floating charge but are disallowed the right to put in a receiver.

- An administrative receiver can be appointed by the debenture holder to sell the assets of the business to the highest bidder; as with administration, shareholders and directors lose control. The receiver's task is to realize the assets at the best price to repay the debenture holder, the balance to pay the other creditors in due preference.
- Very often this means bringing down costs in line with volume to sell the assets as a going concern, with a secondary objective of transferring the maximum number of employees. In a receivership, assets are sold without any liabilities and the creditors are paid depending upon their security in a laid down priority. The

shareholders are the last priority and usually receive nothing.
- Liquidation is the final resort. The assets are sold without necessarily attempting to sell the parts as going concerns.

Penalties faced by banks in keeping businesses alive

There are a number of remedies that a bank can accept with more or less enthusiasm:

- The most usual is to convert short- to long-term debt which takes pressure off management and can allow the company to borrow more when cash flow starts to become positive.
- The bank can insist that it is only prepared to put in new money on condition that shareholders do the same and there is a change of management. The matter can be negotiated directly where there is a large minority shareholder, such as a venture capital company. Where there are many institutional shareholders the merchant bank is seen as the (often reluctant) intermediary.
- In the last resort banks have been obliged to convert debt into equity where there is a good chance either that the company can be rescued or that an asset, such as property, will regain its value in the next economic upturn.

Independent directors' contributions to saving businesses

Unfortunately, bankers and insolvency practitioners have not found independent directors much help in preventing companies going wrong. Many of the companies that failed in the early 1990s had senior and experienced people on their boards who seemed to know little about the business and could not restrain entrepreneurial executives. These are some of the comments made by senior bankers and insolvency practitioners.

Michael Jordan, Chairman and Senior Partner of Cork Gully & Co.

He hopes that gone are the days when an independent director was a friend of the chairman and turned up once a month to nod in agreement and be rewarded with a good lunch. In his opinion the changes have not gone far enough. In some major company failures in the early 1990s, non-executive directors did little or nothing to spot the problems or take remedial action. Particularly when a company is run by an entrepreneur, it is essential for non-executives to understand the accounting systems, and particularly the authority within a group for moving around large sums of money.

In these situations, Jordan believes that independent directors should be 'streetwise'. For example a director may be technically able to understand the board papers, a marketing strategy and participate in discussions over acquisitions or mergers; however, he may be useless in spotting potential pitfalls and anticipating sharp practice by others.

Often board papers lack specific information on cash flow or balance sheet values. This should alert an independent director who must insist on full information. An independent director should understand the financial systems, whose signature is needed for shifting around the group's cash and how it is spent, for example on yachts and aeroplanes. He should also understand much of what is happening at subsidiary level. Finally he should be totally independent and have the courage to speak his mind.

Independent directors' sanctions are limited and, if disgruntled they should not feel free to complain to the media, so likely damaging a company's reputation. They should, however, voice their concerns around the board table and directly to the auditors. The complaints should be minuted. Thereafter, the independent director will be free, with the board's knowledge, to approach the major shareholders or an Investment Committee. This is not universally popular with the Institutions as the receipt of confidential information might make them insiders and so be unable to deal in shares.

Resignation just before insolvency will not protect independent directors. If they are concerned that the company is trading wrongfully they should, after seeking legal advice, bring their protest before the full board. Should their request for a full internal enquiry (including the auditors) not be accepted they should ensure their complaint is minuted before resigning.

Mark Homan, Senior Insolvency Partner, Price Waterhouse & Co.

A well-informed independent director can help a board gain a wider perspective. For example, the length of the 1980s upswing gave many managements a false sense of confidence and they failed to anticipate the downturn which started in 1990.

The euphoria and a climate of intense competition for banks to lend money encouraged entrepreneurs to negotiate loans which totally failed to recognize the potential downside risk. Independent directors should, for example, help the board to acquaint themselves with such matters as the business cycles.

Another facet of the 1980s was a number of acquisitions funded by the banks which were outside the acquirer's core business and beyond the managers' range of experience. The high mortgage rates that typically end the business cycle were not seen as a warning indicator. The correlation between mortgage interest rates, housing sales and consumer spending on household goods in 1989 and 1990 make an interesting study. The downturn affected firms like Magnet supplying doors and window frames, MFI selling flatpack furniture and kitchens and Lowndes Queensway more general furniture.

When the mortgage rates rose quickly in 1989, the housing market died and sales of the companies heavily linked to household expenditure (many of which were highly geared) dropped precipitously. The ensuing losses put the companies rapidly into the bank's intensive-care units. These were companies that had dozens, even hundreds, of bankers. This situation was a major factor in the almost overnight change in outlook in August 1989. This changed the City from domination by marketing bankers to credit controllers!

An independent director's job varies considerably with the type of company. The independent director of a PLC with institutional shareholders can encourage investors to retire a chief executive, which has been done in several cases in the early 1990s. This action is not practically possible in a company where the chief executive is also the majority shareholder, which can put an independent director in a precarious position.

Where possible there has to be a balance around the board table which should include at least someone who was acutely aware what was going on – that might echo Michael Jordan's streetwise director.

Insolvency practitioners might make good independent directors because, along with insolvency lawyers and company doctors, they learn a lot from others' mistakes. But this is just one facet and an ideal board composition should encompass many skills. Homan believes that although the Insolvency Act imposes many penalties on independent directors, their liability has still to be tested in the courts. For example, is it reasonable to expect an independent director or a marketing director spending most of his time overseas to have the same information and responsibility as the chief executive or finance director?

Finally Homan feels that far too much emphasis is placed upon last year's operating statement and balance sheet and too little on the underlying assumptions behind the forward budget. He feels that the board as a whole should come to a balanced judgement about the market conditions in each of the market sectors and decide on an attainable level of volume and costs; they should also work out the sensitivities based on an excess or shortfall. Often an investigating accountant has to recast budgets on a realistic basis from unrealistic assumptions accepted by the board.

John Thomson, Head of Lending and Risk Management, Midland Bank

Thomson's department has found a different style of management is needed for a recession than for boom times, and believes this is beneficial for corporate leadership. Thomson believes that American football team tactics have something to teach management where there are different groups responsible for either offensive or defensive play. His teams are defensive players. When a company is in trouble it should never try to trade out of problems. The correct approach is to rationalize and cut costs to bring the business in line with the market. Some management can be equally good in offence as defence, most cannot. Many also lack the capacity to anticipate the bad times. However good independent directors' skills, they cannot be a substitute for competent executive management.

The Midland experience of independent directors is mixed. In the early 1990s there have been failures with a bevy of independent directors who have not been effective, particularly when the board has been led by an autocratic entrepreneurial figure; in one case, the individual was the sole (and unchallenged by the bank) cheque signatory. There have been other cases in larger companies when the independent directors were ineffective.

The Midland does not, as a policy, interview the independent directors as well as their customers' executives but there are cases when the bank discusses problems with the independent directors when talks with the executives have not been fruitful. However, in some cases, the independent directors have made a contribution, particularly in family controlled firms, when the shareholders have been prepared to listen.

Thomson endorses Jordan's view about the variability of board reports and the need for independent directors to delve deeply should the quality be suspect. An independent director could also make external enquiries, perhaps with customers or suppliers or in the stock market, to learn an outside view of the company.

David Russell, Director of Group Credit Control, National Westminster Bank

Not surprisingly, NatWest's experience of failures is similar to that of the other clearing banks. The major problems have been companies with headstrong market oriented entrepreneurs who have borrowed from a number of banks and often do not know exactly the extent of their gearing. Such managers are often backed by a weak financial team and independent directors who are there more for status than effectiveness and do not question the executives as much as they should. Russell also agrees that to do their job properly, independent directors should learn about the company's business, its systems and not be afraid to seek for the truth.

Russell believes that the Insolvency Act, albeit with some problems, has concentrated the minds of directors on their personal involvement. This is no bad thing. The banks could re-enforce this responsibility by interviewing the whole board, although this has not been popular with the company's executives or their financial advisers. However, when a company is in intensive care the bank can (and does) insist that properly qualified people are on the board as a condition for continuing the facility.

David Turle, Deputy Divisional Director, Barclays Bank

As with other banks, Barclays experience of independent directors is mixed – their contribution in many cases being minimal. Sometimes they have found a good independent director who understands the nature of the business but these have been more the exception than the rule and there seems little point in a board having more independent directors unless the quality is raised.

Barclays do not impose directors, being conscious of the implications of being a 'shadow director'. If board changes are a condition of continuing a facility, they leave it to the company to make their own selection. The bank's greatest recovery successes have been through a partnership between the intensive-care unit and the company executives.

Turle believes that an independent director can only be effective if he is involved in the business and receives quality information. It is recognized that both considerations will be limited by what the executive directors provide and independent directors will need both courage and persistence. Turle cites an example of an independent director who, within two weeks of his company becoming insolvent became deeply concerned, not about the company, but his own position. He clearly had no understanding of the business and in any case, his contribution would have been minimal. However, there have been a few cases where the independent director has been very effective.

17

Views of the Institute of Directors
The board and the non-executive director

Blenyth Jenkins
Director of Corporate Affairs
Institute of Directors

The role of the board

The key role of any board, is to continue and develop profitably the business in the light of changing circumstances, and the effectiveness or otherwise of a board is directly reflected in the growth and operating performance of the business.

It is a truism to say that all companies have a built-in propensity to fail. This is because the perpetual changes which continually reshape the circumstances of a company (call them market forces if you like) tend to undermine yesterday's profitable operations, turning them instead into loss-making tomorrows. It is only by anticipating and reacting to these changes that companies convert the challenge of survival into the opportunity to prosper. The successful control of this process is what distinguishes the management of a business from the administration of a bureaucracy.

A board fulfils its role by the exercise of the following key functions: first, setting the company's strategic direction; second, ensuring its implementation; third, monitoring management; and fourth, providing information regarding the affairs of the company to those entitled to require it.

It will be evident that successful implementation of the exercise of these functions is heavily dependent on the performance of the company's management. This in turn leads to the proposition that, in each case, the effectiveness of the management is influenced by the composition of the board, which should be such as to ensure accountability management and effectiveness.

Composition of the board

In considering the composition of the board, it should be noted that the system of corporate governance in Britain does not have an effective mechanism providing for the external accountability of company managements. While at law, the shareholders have the right to elect and remove directors, in practice this right is seldom exercised in order to enforce accountability. While, in the case of well-run companies, this lack of external accountability may not be thought to be important, there are a number of issues in relation to which potential conflicts of interest can arise between the management and the other stakeholders in the company. Examples are defence against hostile takeover, executive remuneration, the company's diversification, or indeed the very competence of the company's management.

In addition to these specific instances of potential conflict of interest there is, of course, an inherent general conflict of interest in the position of the executive directors sitting on a board, one of whose prime functions is to monitor their own performance in their capacity as executives. They are in effect monitoring themselves and, as we have seen, with very little in the way of external accountability.

In these circumstances it is for the companies themselves to introduce their own system of accountability by the presence on their board of independent non-executive directors. While the present legal framework in this country permits the appointment of boards of directors consisting entirely of executive directors, it is generally accepted that the presence of non-executive directors ensures that there is built-in to the board structure a system of checks and balances to ensure that an objective view is brought to bear in cases of potential conflicts of interest.

This is particularly the case in relation to public companies, where it is widely accepted that there should be a minimum of three non-executive directors, or one-third of the total for larger companies or two or one-quarter of the total for smaller companies. However, the same considerations apply to any private company, large or small, which wishes to ensure the integrity of its board's operations. The relevance of non-executive directors to different types of company will be returned to later in this chapter.

Function of non-executive directors

In providing the element of accountability to company boards, the non-executive director may be expected to contribute in three specific areas and the contribution of the non-executive director does, in fact, extend beyond the accountability role. All boards of directors differ in their manner of operation, but the following three functions of the non-executive director are of general application.

First, the non-executive director should take responsibility for monitoring management performance and the extent to which the management of the company is achieving the results planned when strategy was determined. It is for the board to establish the company's strategy and the non-executive director has a key role in this process. Thereafter, the board has to ensure implementation of the strategic plan and monitor management performance in its execution. In this process the executive directors are wearing two hats, as directors they are monitors and as executives they are being monitored. The dichotomy involved in the exercise of this dual function is clearly a source of tension if not of actual conflict of interest, so any board will be immeasurably strengthened in exercising this function by the injection into board proceedings of the independence and objectivity of its non-executive directors.

The second aspect of the function of the non-executive director is to ensure that the board has adequate systems to safeguard the interests of the company where these may conflict with the personal interests of individual directors. Examples are areas such as board appointments and remuneration and ensuring the presentation of adequate financial information. This role is generally fulfilled through the use of committees of the board, to which executive directors cannot be appointed on the grounds of perceived self-interest, in relation to which therefore the presence of non-executive directors is of fundamental importance. Three such committees are now becoming increasingly common, the audit, remuneration, and nominating committees. Respectively they are responsible for ensuring a direct line of communication between the auditors and the whole board; deciding the remuneration of executive directors (including the chairman and chief executive); and nominating new candidates for election to the board.

Third, while the negative or 'watchdog' element of the function of a non-executive director has rightly been emphasized, this is totally to ignore the positive benefits that are derived from the presence on a board of non-executive directors. While there is no reason in law why a board should not be composed entirely of executive directors, there is always a danger of such a board becoming inbred, lacking both the wider perspectives and the domestic stimuli to perform which an external presence might provide. In other words, a glorified management committee, managing, as opposed to directing, the business. The presence of non-executives on a board introduces two elements which cannot be provided by a purely executive board, namely independence and objectivity. Independence in that the non-executive director has no subordinate executive status to either the chairman or the chief executive and objectivity in that, having no executive function he has no personal commitment to any particular strategic option prepared by the executives for consideration by the board. Consequently the impact of the non-executive directors' contributions to the board proceedings, and one of the basic functions of the role, is to widen the horizons within which the board determines strategy, both by applying the fruits of a wider general experience and by bringing into board discussions any background of special skill knowledge and experience which is relevant to strategy and which the board might otherwise lack. However, the key to the effective application of these attributes is the non-executive's special position, which enables him to do so in an independent and objective manner.

It is appropriate, at this juncture, to note that, just as there is a duality in the role of the executive director in that he both monitors and is monitored, there exists a similar potential conflict within the role of the non-executive director in that he is both monitor of management performance and is himself a decision maker upon which management performance is based. In other words, he is both responsible (along with his executive colleagues) for making decisions and is, at the same time, charged with assessing the performance of the executives in the making of such decisions. Under the unitary board concept which obtains in this country all directors, whether executive or non-executive, bear equal responsibility for the direction of the company and the non-executive director is not a concept recognized within our legal system. The non-executive director bears equal responsibility with his executive colleagues in relation to decisions of the board on which by definition they are likely to be better informed than he is.

There is no ready solution to this conundrum. The proposal that we should adopt a two-tier board system creating a clear split between directors and managers is one that runs contrary to the corporate culture of this country and also cuts across the concept of a director as being a specific professional function, totally distinct from that of a manager or a delegate of shareholders or bankers. In these circumstances, it is imperative that the affairs of the board be arranged in such a way that non-executive directors are involved at the earliest possible stage in the decision-making process and that they are supplied at all stages with adequate and timely information regarding the financial situation of the company and other matters likely to influence board decisions.

Appointment of non-executive directors

In the light of the potential significance of the contribution of the non-executive director, the appointment process should be taken with the utmost seriousness by the board making the appointment.

An appointment to the board is not a matter lightly to be undertaken, and it requires full commitment on the part of the existing board. The role of nomination committees in making recommendations for appointments has previously been noted, but whether or not a nomination committee exists, (and in the case of smaller companies the existence of such a committee may not be appropriate), the appointment process should embrace features in common.

Selection

The company should prepare a detailed brief on the existing board, together with its objectives. By way of complement to this, the board should give careful consideration to the attributes and skills they are seeking, together with the features they would regard as being inappropriate in the proposed appointee.

In so doing the board should consider the attributes required of a non-executive director. These are:

1 *Independence*. This may be defined as not having any contractual relationship with the company or its directors and not being subject to any control or influence of a third party which could affect the exercise of independent judgement.
2 *Commitment*. In addition to making himself available for board meetings, the non-executive director plays a key role in serving on various committees of the board and his availability to serve on such committees is a matter very much to be taken into account in the selection process. Over and above attendance at formal meetings, however, is the requirement that the non-executive director should ensure that he is able to familiarize himself with the company, its business and procedures and to acquaint himself with the management of the company. Additionally, he must, of course, keep himself up to date on these matters. Without such commitment, his contribution at formal meetings is likely to be limited, and the time required to involve himself in the affairs of the company in this way is often underestimated.
3 *Motivation*. The non-executive director should be motivated not by the prestige of serving on a particular board, the status of being a director, nor the financial rewards on offer, (as this is

likely to erode independence if it operates as a primary motivation), nor as a means of keeping occupied after retirement. The primary motivation of the non-executive director should be a wish to make a contribution to the affairs of the company, to which may quite legitimately be added a desire to broaden his own personal experience, in involving himself in the direction of a company other than his own. Many company chairmen encourage their executives to accept non-executive directorships in other companies, on the basis that this also has the effect of enlarging the perspective the director concerned is then able to bring to bear on the affairs of his own company.

4 *Experience*. It is imperative that a non-executive director has experience of top level management, that he knows how companies work and the respective roles of the board and of management. The field in which this experience has been gained is not necessarily relevant as his contribution may be more valuable if his experience complements rather than duplicates that of the other directors.

5 *Communication skills*. To operate effectively the non-executive director must work as part of a team consisting of the chairman and the other board members. In order to perform in this role he must have the ability to communicate, to express clearly his opinions, to persuade others and to defend his position in the case of disagreement. Contribution to boardroom discussion is one of the criteria by which a non-executive director is judged and it is fundamental to the role of the non-executive director that he should be able to make this contribution in a positive and constructive manner and in such a way as not to have the effect of antagonizing his colleagues on the board.

6 *Impartiality*. While being a full participant in board discussions the non-executive director should disassociate himself from any factions that may arise among executive directors and should be prepared to demonstrate independence of mind in the face of any factions that do arise. Similarly, the non-executive director should consider the interests of all stakeholders in the business, shareholders, employees, suppliers, customers and the community at large and should demonstrably do so in an objective manner.

7 *Integrity*. Fundamental to good corporate governance is the integrity of the board's proceedings and the maintenance of the highest ethical and business standards throughout the company.

The non-executive director should contribute to the maintenance of these standards.

Procedure

Having, as it were, settled the specification, the board should then determine the mechanics. A member or members of the board should be designated as 'owning' the search process and the method of search should be determined. In this connection, it should be noted that the majority of non-executive director appointments are made on the basis of personal acquaintance, either to the board generally or to the chairman. While there is, of course, no reason why an appointment made on this basis should not operate effectively, we have seen that two of the key attributes of non-executive director are independence and objectivity and too close a personal connection may lead to an erosion of these attributes. Indeed, a well-known company chairman recently remarked that a prime qualification of a potential non-executive director was that he should *not* be personally known to the chairman! Consideration should therefore be given to widening the field of search, by the use either of recruitment consultants or by consulting one of the two organizations specializing in providing suitably qualified candidates for appointment as non-executive directors, the Institute of Directors (as part of its wider function), or Pro Ned.

In acknowledging the crucial importance of any board appointment, the board should accept that there will be a cost factor, both direct, if outside agencies are involved, and indirect, in terms of management time. There is not the slightest merit in rushing into hasty commitments and the directors entrusted with the search process should proceed in a selective manner, governed by the guidelines previously established by the board as a whole. An important part of this process is to ensure that none of the proposed candidates has any conflict of interest, actual or potential, through other business interests.

When the search process has proceeded to the extent of producing a short list of potential candidates, the directors concerned should give the board as a whole the opportunity of meeting those on the short list – not in any sense as a form of interview, but an equal status. In this way, the whole of the board will be involved in the final appointment, and difficult questions of personal chemistry between potential board colleagues will have been avoided.

Letter of appointment

A decision having been made, it is highly advisable that the newly appointed non-executive director be issued with a letter of appointment. This need not be in any sense a formal agreement, but should clearly establish the position on a number of issues which, if not clarified at the outset, could lead to subsequent embarrassment. In particular, there are four matters as to which both parties need to be absolutely clear right from the outset of the relationship.

First, there is the question of defining precisely what is required of the new non-executive director. In addition to meetings of the board and their frequency, are there board committees on which he is required to serve? Are these outside the formal structure, such as strategic planning conferences, which he will be required to attend? Will it be necessary for him to visit company locations other than head office? Is foreign travel involved? Misunderstanding on any of these points can lead to disruption of meetings, through absences, or indeed result in the non-executive director deciding that the degree of commitment required was greater than expected, thus prompting his resignation.

Second, the fees involved should be clearly specified. While, as we have seen, the desire for financial reward should not be a primary motivating factor of a non-executive director, the embarrassment of a possible misunderstanding on this score is clearly to be avoided, and the amount of the fee, method and date of payment and frequency of review should be specified in the letter of appointment.

Third, expenses. While non-executive directors are entitled to be reimbursed for expenses necessarily incurred in performance of their duties, this should be reinforced by an indemnification provision in the Articles of Association, which should be widely enough drawn to extend to the cost of legal or other advice or other expenditure incurred by a non-executive director or group of non-executive directors in relation to the performance of their duties, and independently of the company. The question of liabilities not covered by this indemnity, i.e. those arising from negligence default or breach of trust should also be considered, and the position as to whether such liabilities are covered by insurance, arranged either by the company or privately, should clearly be established.

Fourth, while the Articles of Association will contain provision for election and re-election of directors by the shareholders, there is considerable merit in specifying in the letter of appointment a specific period of office, rather than allowing this to be open-ended. There is, of course, no reason why the original term should not, at its expiration be extended, if both parties so agree, but the presence of a cut-off point obviates embarrassment if, at that juncture, either party feels it would not be in their interest for an extension of office to be made.

Induction

Finally, in relation to appointment, the company should arrange an induction programme for the newly appointed non-executive director. In addition to the provision of the most recent board and relevant committee minutes, financial statements and board authorities, this should comprise introductory visits to the heads of the key functions within the company and, where appropriate outside advisers such as auditors. The induction programme, to be successful, must be taken seriously by both company and newly appointed director, as its success or otherwise can often determine the director's relationship with the company, and vice versa, throughout his term of office.

The role of the non-executive director in different types of company

It is sometimes assumed that the relevance of non-executive directors is confined to the boards of large quoted companies, and it is true that just as these large companies have a higher public profile than smaller companies, so the role of the non-executive director in such companies tends to receive greater public attention. Also, the committee structure of the board, in relation to which the non-executive director has a vital part to play is perhaps more appropriate for the larger company. Finally, in quoted companies the non-executive director has a significant role in assuring shareholders of the integrity of the board's operations. In this connection, it should be noted that this does not mean, as has been claimed in some quarters, that non-executive directors have 'a special responsibility' in relation to the shareholders. Under the unitary board system which obtains in this country all directors have equal responsibility, and it is simply not the case that any group of directors has a greater responsibility, legal or otherwise, for any aspect of the company's activities.

However, while the impact of non-executives on the boards of larger companies is generally acknowledged, less widely appreciated is the positive contribution that can be made to the running of medium sized and small companies through the presence of non-executive directors on the board. Quite apart from the injection into board proceedings of the key elements of independence and objectivity previously mentioned, a non-executive director may be expected to contribute to the effectiveness of the board of a small or medium sized company in ways that do not perhaps operate in the case of larger companies.

Put in another way, while in larger quoted companies, the appointment of non-executive directors tends to be motivated by a desire to strengthen the board in performance of its monitoring or governance functions, in smaller companies the emphasis of such appointments is to widen the board's horizons, in bringing to the board a perspective not present among its existing members.

First, there is a tendency, particularly in smaller companies, for the board meetings to be spent managing rather than directing. The vital distinction here is that direction is the formulation of policy and managing, following from direction, is the implementation of that policy. Such a board will tend to operate on a day-to-day basis, reacting to events rather than pursuing policies leading to the attainment of the company's objectives. The non-executive director does not have management responsibilities and is therefore focused on the direction of the business as opposed to its management, and it is a prime contribution of a non-executive director to help his executive colleagues think like directors rather than like managers so that the company operates according to a thought-out policy rather than on a day-to-day basis.

Second, it is fundamental to a board's effectiveness that it be provided with accurate current and complete information. The mere fact of the appointment is likely to lead to an improvement in the quality of this information, as the papers then have to be prepared in such a manner as to be comprehensible to someone not involved with the running of the business on a daily basis. However, over and above what may be termed this passive factor, the non-executive director can make a significant positive contribution in criticizing the quality and adequacy of the information being made available and making suggestions for its improvement.

Third, and allied to the previous point, is the role of the non-executive director in relation to the system of financial controls operating within the company. The quality of financial information coming before the board is, of course, dependent on the efficacy of such systems and, in view of his potential personal liability, the non-executive director will have a particular interest in ensuring their adequacy. This has assumed much greater significance in the light of the provisions of the Insolvency Act 1986.

Fourth, and this is perhaps the most obvious, a non-executive director can bring outside business experience to the board and, in some cases, technical expertise in areas where the board is weak.

Fifth, finally, and of particular significance for the smaller company, the non-executive directors will always have the interests of the company at heart when going about is other outside activities, e.g. new business for manufacturers, new accounts with sales and distribution companies, foreign opportunities, and a whole host of benefits not seen as part of the original arrangements.

Conclusion

I hope it will be obvious from the foregoing that the role of the non-executive director is a challenging one, but it is also a rewarding one. To operate effectively it requires a firm commitment both from the company and from the director himself. When it operates effectively, the role adds a significant extra dimension to the direction of the company, both in terms of broadening the board's perspective in considering policy issues and in providing the checks and balances on the executive necessary to ensure the integrity of the board's proceedings.

References and further reading

Alderfer, C. P. (1986) The Invisible Director on Corporate Boards, *Harvard Business Review*.

Ansoff, H. I. (1965) *Corporate Strategy*. Penguin

Argenti, J. (1976) *Practical Corporate Planning*. Unwin Hyman

Argenti, J. (1976) *Corporate Collapse*. McGraw-Hill

Association of British Insurers (1991) *Role and Duties of Directors*. ABI

Baskin, O. and Aronoff, C. (1991) *Public Relations*. William C Brown

Benton, P. F. (1991) *Riding the Whirlwind*. Blackwell

Cadbury, A. (1990) *The Company Chairman*. IOD and Woodhead-Faulkner

Coopers & Lybrand Deloitte (undated) *Becoming a Director?* In assocation with Cork Gully

Corporate Renewal Associates (undated) *Governance*. Corporate Renewal Associates, Fitzroy Square, London

Davies, A. H. T. (1991) *Strategic Leadership*. Woodhead-Faulkner in association with the IOD

Economist Intelligence Unit (1990) *Non Executive Directors – Their changing role on UK boards*. Economist Publications

Franks, J. A. (1990) *The Company Director and the Law*. Longman

Gouldnes, Solicitors (1989) *Guide to D & O Liability and Loss Prevention*. Special Risk Services

Greener, T. (1991) *Secrets of Successful Public Relations and Image-making*. Butterworth-Heinemann

Hargreaves, R. (1983) *Starting a business*. Butterworth-Heinemann

Harvey-Jones, J. (1988) *Making It Happen*. Mandarin

Harvey-Jones, J. (1991) *Getting It Together*. Mandarin

Houlden, B. (1990) *Understanding Company Strategy*. Blackwell

Houston, W. (1989) *Avoiding Adversity*. David & Charles

Houston, W. (1991) *How You Can Profit from the Recession*. Scope Books

Institute of Chartered Accountants in England & Wales (1991) *The Changing Role of the Non-Executive Director*. ICAEW

Institute of Directors (1991) *Code of Practice for the Non-Executive Director*. IOD

Institute of Directors (1991) *Guidelines for Directors*. IOD

Institute of Directors and Norwich Union (1991) *Director's Guide to Company Insurance*. The Director Publications

Insurance Institute of London (1986) *Directors and Officers Liability Insurance Report*. Advanced Study Group No. 226

Johnson, G. and Scholes, K. (1989) *Exploring Company Strategy*. Prentice Hall

Kotler, R. (1991) *Principles of Marketing*. Prentice Hall

Linden-Travers, K. (1990) *Non-Executive Directors*. IOD and Woodhead-Faulkner

Loose, P. and Yelland, J. (1987) *The Company Director – His Functions, Powers and Duties*. Jordans in association with IOD

Merton Associates (1991) *Non-Executive Directors of 70 PLCs*. Merton Associates, Grafton Way, London

McCarthur, C. and Barnard I. (1988) *Company Director's Guide to the Law*. Waterlow

Mills, G. (1981) *On the Board*. Allen and Unwin

Norburn, D. (1989) The British Boardroom: Time for a Revolution? *Long Range Planning*.

Parker, H. (1990) *Letters to a New Chairman*. IOD and Woodhead-Faulkner

Parker, H. (1990). *Long Range Planning*, vol. 23, no. 4

Peters, T. (1987) *Thriving on Chaos*. Pan

Peters, T. and Waterman, R. (1982) *In Search of Excellence*. Harper and Row

Porter, M. (1980) *Competitive Strategy*. Free Press

Pro Ned (1990) *A Practical Guide for Non-Executive Directors*. Pro Ned London

Pro Ned (1990) *The Code of Recommended Practice for Non-Executive Directors*. Pro Ned London

Pro Ned (1990) *Remuneration Committees: A Survey of Current Practice 1990.* Pro Ned London

Ryan, C. L. (1988) *Company Directors: Liabilities, Rights and Duties.* CCH Editions

Sealy, L. S. (1988) *Disqualification and Personal Liability of Directors.* CCH Editions

Souster, P. (1990) *The Director's Responsibilities and Liabilites.* Institute of Chartered Accountants in England & Wales

Taylor, B. and Tricker, R. (1990) *The Director's Manual.* IOD and Woodhead-Faulkner

Taylor, B. (1991) *Strategic Planning: The Chief Executive and the Board.* Pergamon Press

Titmuss, Sainer and Webb, Solicitors (1990) *Shadow Directorship and the Banker.* Special Risk Services

Wright, D. (1987) *Rights and Duties of Directors.* Butterworths

Yip, G. (1988) *Barriers to Entry: A Corporate Strategy Perspective.* Lexington Books

Index